# THE SUSTAINING POWER OF HOPE

# THE SUSTAINING POWER OF
# HOPE

## Leslie B. Flynn

While this book is designed for the reader's personal enjoyment and profit, it is also intended for group study. A Leader's Guide with Victor Multiuse Transparency Masters is available from your local bookstore or from the publisher.

*From The Library of Greg Cheatham*

**BOOKS** a division of SP Publications, Inc.
WHEATON, ILLINOIS 60187

*Offices also in*
Whitby, Ontario, Canada
Amersham-on-the-Hill, Bucks, England

Unless otherwise noted, Scripture quotations
are from the *King James Version*. Other quotations
are from the *New International Version* (NIV),
© 1973, 1978, 1984 by the International Bible
Society, and used by permission of Zondervan
Bible Publishers; *The Holy Bible: Revised Standard
Version* (RSV), © 1952 by the Division of Christian
Education of the National Council of the
Churches of Christ in the United States; *The
Living Bible* (TLB), © 1971 by Tyndale House; and
*The New Testament in Modern English* (PH),
© 1958, 1960, 1972 by J.B. Phillips, Macmillan
Publishing Co., Inc. Used by permission.

Recommended Dewey Decimal Classification: 248
Suggested Subject Heading: FAITH

Library of Congress Catalog Card Number: 85-50321
ISBN: 0-89693-600-7

© 1985 by SP Publications, Inc. All rights reserved
Printed in the United States of America

VICTOR BOOKS
A division of SP Publications, Inc.
Wheaton, Illinois 60187

# CONTENTS

1. HOPE—YOU CAN'T LIVE WITHOUT IT
   9

2. WHAT IS HOPE?
   19

3. WHERE DO WE GO FOR HOPE?
   29

4. THE BELIEVER'S GUARANTEED HOPE
   41

5. THE THERAPY OF HOPE
   52

6. DASHED HOPES
   63

7. HOPE OF A SECOND CHANCE
   71

8. HOPE IN THE FACE OF DEATH
   81

9. THE BLESSED HOPE
   91

10. THE FOUNTAIN OF YOUTH
    101

11. HOW TO GIVE HOPE TO OTHERS
    111

12. HOPE OF HARVEST
    122

*To my congregation
at Grace Conservative Baptist Church
in Nanuet, New York,
who for over 36 years
have given my wife and me
encouragement and hope*

# ONE
# HOPE—YOU CAN'T LIVE WITHOUT IT

**KIDS PREDICT NUCLEAR DESTRUCTION**

I Spotted That Headline on a local newspaper in Mexico recently.

The accompanying story told how over half of a sixth-grade class, questioned on the outcome of another world war, said, "It would blow up the entire earth." This class consisted of six Americans, nine Mexicans, two Britishers, and one student each from Switzerland, France, Peru, Korea, India, and Brazil.

Even very young children worry about nuclear war. Likewise, many adults worry when they realize that before long many small nations with potentially trigger-fingered fanatic governments will also possess such weapons.

Nations stagger from one crisis to another. One quarter of the world is at war. Approximately 10,000 people a week die of starvation. Millions are without sufficient daily food, without shelter, without medical care, and without liberty.

Some experts predict that non-renewable resources will be exhausted within a century. In its sobering report, *The Limits of Growth,* the Club of Rome (an elite international organization of economists and scientists) predicts that under ideal conditions industrial growth can continue only a short while, to be followed by inevitable collapse.

The certainty and finality of death casts a raiment of hopelessness over many. A world traveler commented, "I have seen burials in all parts of the globe. I have seen Orientals throw their corpses out in the field for the animals to devour. I have seen Hindus take their dead to the burning ghats. I have seen others take the bodies to the roof of their temple where the vultures swooped down on them. I have seen an African throw the body of his wife or child into a river. All did so without any assurance of seeing their loved ones again. They sang no hymn of hope, but chanted only dirges of despair."

## Hope—A Neglected Subject

In an article in *Christianity Today,* Dr. Armand Mayo Nicholi II of Harvard Medical School says, "The word 'hope' is used and heard little in our culture. Perhaps hope conflicts with our concept of a scientific world. Many books exist on faith and on love, but few on hope. Psychiatrist Karl Menninger writes, 'In scientific circles there is a determined effort to exclude hope from conceptual thinking . . . because of a fear of corrupting objective judgment by wishful thinking. But all science is built on hope, so much so that science is for many moderns a substitute for religion. . . . Man can't help hoping even if he is a scientist. He can only hope more accurately' " ("Why Can't I Deal with Depression?" *Christianity Today,* November 11, 1983).

A syndicated newspaper columnist recently asserted that the study of hope is an area "very much undeveloped in psychology." The writer went on to say that hope, that elusive feeling that lifts the spirit against seemingly insurmountable odds, is now the focus of scientific investigation (Sally Squires, *Newhouse News Science,* April 5, 1984).

**Hope Is Necessary**
Hope is essential to sanity and a balanced outlook on life. Hope sustains the shipwrecked sailor through long days when no ship sails in sight. Hope spurs the soldier to keep on with the battle even against overwhelming odds. Hope of parole upholds the prisoner in his lonely cell as he checks off the days, months, and years he has served on his homemade calendar.

People with long-term problems need hope. So do people with shattering losses, whether of health, job, or marriage.

Neoorthodox theologian Emil Brunner said, "What oxygen is for the lungs, such is hope for the meaning of human life. Take oxygen away and death occurs through suffocation; take hope away and humanity is constricted through lack of breath: despair supervenes, spelling the paralysis of intellectual and spiritual powers by a feeling of the senselessness and purposelessness of existence. As the fate of the human organism is dependent on the supply of oxygen, so the fate of humanity is dependent on its supply of hope" (*Eternal Hope,* Westminster Press, p. 11).

In the midst of the proclamations of punishment immediately after man's fall, God also gave hope (Gen. 3:15). Though the ground would be cursed with thorns to impede man's agricultural pursuits, God gave the first prediction of His Son, whose head would be crowned with thorns, as He sacrificed Himself to redeem us from sin's curse.

**Don Baker**
Don Baker, well-known pastor and author, was being led down the silent halls of a psychiatric ward in an Oregon

hospital. A fervent preacher, capable counselor, and delightful socializer, he had often found himself, without warning, overcome by periods of weakness and depression. Overwhelmed with feelings of inadequacy, occasionally he had toyed with thoughts of self-destruction. After collapsing in convulsive sobs one Sunday morning, he agreed to seek competent psychiatric care.

Part of the admission process involved filling out forms and depositing his jewelry and other valuables. Waiting in line, he heard a familiar voice say, "Next." The admitting nurse was one of his own church members. With disbelief on her face she asked, "Pastor, what are you doing. . . ?" Her voice trailed into silence as she recognized what was happening.

In the following days, various staff members of the hospital probed with gentle questions: How do you feel? Do you sleep well? How do you feel about your job? About yourself? About your family? Do you have difficulties making decisions? Do you like to be around people? Are you often angry? Ever thought of suicide? Baker's answers indicated wrong attitudes in all those areas. Only graphic memories of seeing so many shattered lives in the wake of suicide kept him from taking his own life.

Then one day a wise counselor, after probing with more questions, gently said, "I'm sure, Mr. Baker, that the doctor's diagnosis is correct. You are deeply depressed. You *do* need to be here. But you'll get better. It will take time, but you'll get better."

Says Baker, "I'll always be grateful for those gentle words—profound in their simplicity—yet filled with hope. And oh, how I needed hope. For one brief moment there was a slight glimmer of light in my black hole of depression. Not enough to illuminate the many unanswered questions. Not even enough to plot a future, but there was light. It was just enough to enable me to make out the word—Hope. I fondled and nurtured that word. I cradled it in every waking moment. It was the only word that sustained me through the interminable nights punctuated with endless interruptions and the oftentimes meaningless days filled with frantic activity" (Donald Baker and Emery Nester, *Depression: Finding Hope and Meaning in Life's Darkest Shadow,* Multnomah Press, p. 23).

His wife's first visit was difficult for both. But as he held her in his arms, he could only think of one thing to say. "I'll get better. It may take time, but I'll get better."

One of the doctors suggested Baker's symptoms seemed to indicate hypoglycemia as part of his problem; he prescribed a diet which brought Baker's weight down to normal. Don Baker found himself walking the long hall of Ward 7-E with restrained hopefulness. Ten weeks after admittance, he was released.

Resigning his church, he wondered if his career was over. Visiting churches as a worshiper with his family, pastor-friends would often greet him with embarrassment, not knowing what to do or say. A few months later, Baker became the pastor of the Hinson Memorial Baptist Church in Portland, Oregon. In the years of his ministry there, over 2,500 new members were added, attendance tripled, offerings increased five times, and nearly 100 of the youth either entered foreign missionary service or prepared for it. In addition, the church gave birth to two new congregations, each with more than 300 people in attendance. Baker has since become the pastor of a large church in Rockford, Illinois.

People laughingly commented, "God took a dead man, married him to a dead church, and brought about a resurrection of both."

Baker tells this story in *Depression: Finding Hope and Meaning in Life's Darkest Shadow* (Multnomah Press). Asked why he wrote the book, he replied, "I have shared a painful part of my past with you in the hope that you who stand beside a person trapped in his own black hole might understand, be patient.

loving, and especially careful not to be judgmental or indifferent. And my desire for you who suffer in this darkest shadow of life is that you will be able to identify with some part of it and find hope. Remember—you will get better" (Baker and Nester, *Depression,* pp. 110-111).

### Viktor Frankl

In his book, *Man's Search for Meaning,* Viennese psychiatrist Viktor Frankl has given us a moving account of his grim three years in concentration camps. He tells of the necessity of hope for survival. Like most camp inmates, he suffered from swollen legs and skin so tightly stretched that he could barely bend his knees. He had to leave his shoes unlaced to make them fit his swollen feet. There was no space for socks even if he had had any. His partly bare feet were always wet and his shoes always full of snow, causing frostbite and chills.

Frankl related how starvation reduced inmates to skeletons covered with skin and rags. Unimaginable struggles waged inside men who, digging in a trench, listened only for the siren to announce the half-hour lunch interval when bread would be rationed as long as it was available. While he labored, Frankl kept touching and stroking a piece of bread in his pocket, breaking off a crumb, putting it in his mouth, then with a last ounce of willpower pocketing the rest, vowing to hold off eating it until later.

One day, almost in tears from the pain in his feet due to torn shoes, he limped a few kilometers to the work site with a long column of other prisoners. As he struggled along, he kept thinking of the endless little problems of his miserable life. What would there be to eat that night? If a piece of sausage, should he exchange it for a piece of bread? How could he secure a piece of wire to replace the tiny scrap that served as one of his shoelaces?

## HOPE—YOU CAN'T LIVE WITHOUT IT

Growing disgusted with having to think almost every moment on trivial matters, Frankl forced his mind to another subject. Suddenly he imagined himself standing on a platform in a well-lit, warm lecture hall. To an attentive audience on comfortable, cushioned seats, he was lecturing on the psychology of the concentration camps. He was able to rise above the sufferings of the moment by picturing them as already past. Hope lifted his spirits.

Frankl observed that the prisoner who lost faith in his future also let himself decline and surrender to mental and physical decay. A fellow inmate told Frankl that he had dreamed the war would end by a certain date about a month away. He was full of hope and convinced his dream would be fulfilled. But as the promised date drew nearer and the news reaching the camp made it appear very unlikely he would be free on the promised date, the fellow prisoner suddenly became ill and ran a high temperature. On the promised date he became delirious and lost consciousness. Next day, he was dead. By all outward appearances, he had died of typhus. But close associates knew his sudden loss of hope had lowered his body's resistance against the typhus infection.

As more evidence of the dooming nature of hopelessness, Frankl pointed out the high increase in the death rate between Christmas and New Year in 1944 in that camp. The explanation was not meager rations, colder weather, widespread epidemic, or harder working conditions. Simply, prisoners had lived in the naive hope that they would be home by Christmas. As the holiday approached then passed without a glimmer of good news, despair of future release enveloped them, dangerously lowering their resistance, so that a large number died.

When Frankl was taken to the Auschwitz concentration camp, guards confiscated a manuscript he had been writing. Frankl is convinced that his deep concern to rewrite this book helped him survive the severities of the camp When he came down with typhus fever, he jotted down on little scraps of paper many notes pertaining to the manuscript, should he live to the day of liberation. He wrote, "I am sure that this reconstruction of my lost manuscript in the dark barracks of a Bavarian concentration camp assisted me in overcoming the danger of collapse" (Viktor E. Frankl, *Man's Search for Meaning*, Washington Square Press, p. 165). As the oft-quoted saying goes, "He who has a *why* to live can bear with almost any *how*."

### Christian Hope

Apart from the Christian faith, there is really no guaranteed hope. Despair hangs like a pallor over our world. But the Christian faith offers hope in this life and in the life to come.

The strength of the Christian hope is accentuated by the difference in epitaphs marking the tombs of first-century Christians and unbelievers. Along the Appian Way, which runs south from Rome, stand the disintegrating tombs of aristocratic families that fed on the fat of Rome's power. Inscriptions reflect the barrenness of hope. The crumbling Latin on one stone reads: *What I ate and drank I have with me; what I have left I have lost.* Another says: *A cocktail, please, for you and me.* Still another: *Wine and lust ruin the constitution, but they make life, farewell.*

The early Christians persecuted in the Roman coliseum and arenas were forced to pray below the ground in the catacombs. Excavations in Rome have revealed some 60 catacombs, containing 600 miles of galleries, 8 feet high, and from 3 to 5 feet wide. On both sides are several rows of long, low, horizontal recesses, one above the other like berths on a boat, closed at the front either by a marble slab or by painted tile. Both pagans and Christians buried their dead in these catacombs, but what a difference in epitaphs.

Pagan inscriptions read:

## HOPE—YOU CAN'T LIVE WITHOUT IT

- Live for the present hour, since we are sure of nothing else.
- I will lift my hands against the gods who took me away at the age of 20, though I had done no harm.
- Once I was not. I know nothing about it, and it is no concern of mine.
- Traveler, curse me not as you pass, for I am in darkness and cannot answer.

But when Christian graves were opened, skeletons revealed heads severed from bodies, ribs broken, bones calcined from fire. What a contrast to heathen sentiments to read the epitaphs on the Christians' tombs:

- Here lies Marcia, put to rest in a dream of peace.
- Called away, he went in peace.
- Victorious in peace and in Christ.

A while back ABC-TV aired a controversial program called "The Day After." This vision of nuclear Armageddon depicted a four-minute holocaust in which bombs fell, white light covered the sky over Kansas, then a blinding yellow light flashed, followed by a mushrooming cloud, fire storms, and wind. Buildings exploded and imploded. A poplar forest bent. People became vaporized images on the TV screen. Victims of both bombs and radiation sickness were buried in mass graves.

As the screen went blank, a voice echoed, "Is anybody there? Anybody at all?" Then the same music which opened the program was again heard at the end. It was the tune of the old hymn, "How Firm a Foundation." Though only the tune was heard, this hymn has words of hope most significant to this TV production:

> When through fiery trials thy pathway shall lie,
> My grace, all sufficient, shall be thy supply;
> The flames shall not hurt thee, I only design
> Thy dross to consume, and thy gold to refine.

## THE SUSTAINING POWER OF HOPE

> The soul that on Jesus hath leaned for repose,
> I will not, I will not desert to his foes;
> That soul, though all hell should endeavor to shake,
> I'll never—no, never—no, never forsake!

The same night "The Day After" was aired, one Christian broadcaster ran an evangelistic commercial on his TV network, directed to those who might have switched by chance to his channel. Viewers were invited to call a number for a message of hope, not found in civil defense or nuclear arsenals. Those who phoned in heard that ultimate hope centers in Jesus Christ, the Resurrection and the Life, who has conquered death, and who has promised His followers, "Because I live, ye shall live also" (John 14:19).

# 🐚 TWO 🐚
# WHAT IS HOPE?

An Art Gallery displayed the familiar painting of a lady, representing hope, precariously perched on a sphere, trying to play a harp on which all strings are broken, except one. And she is blindfolded. Two charwomen, cleaning the art gallery, approached the painting. Mused one, "I wonder why they call her hope." Replied the other, "Perhaps it's because she hopes she won't fall off!"

Though this comment may seem somewhat irreverent to the aesthetically minded, it does highlight the ambiguity that surrounds the meaning of hope. What is hope?

Webster's *New Collegiate Dictionary* defines hope as "desire accompanied by expectation of or belief in fulfillment." Or in its verb form, "to cherish a desire with expectation of fulfillment."

**Five Aspects of Hope**
*More Than Wish or Optimism.* Common parlance uses hope to mean *wish*. On the way to a banquet we say, "I hope they serve

roast beef." Driving to the airport, someone sighs, "I hope the plane is on time." Genuine hope goes far beyond wishing.

Real hope extends beyond optimism, which so often is shallow, subjective, and far removed from reality. The tendency of optimistic people is to blindly project their Pollyanna outlook onto life in general. But hope involves more than cheerful optimism, stupid confidence, or positive attitude based on some illusory vision of utopia. The difference between a pipedream and a hope is that the latter has a basis for realization.

*Strong Desire.* Hope is something strongly desired. In hope, the sick man wishes desperately to recover, the hungry to find food, the refugee to find a new homeland, and the prisoner to be released.

Paul wrote to the Romans, "I have longed for many years to come to you. I hope to see you in passing as I go to Spain" (Rom. 15:24, RSV). John expressed his desire to see his readers, "I hope to see you soon, and we will talk together face to face" (3 John 14, RSV).

*Expectation of Fulfillment.* Said Mike after Pat's death, "I hope to meet Pat in heaven, but I don't expect to." This comment revealed not only Mike's true opinion about Pat, but his lack of understanding about the true nature of hope. Hope involves confidence in future fulfillment.

Some Old Testament nouns for hope are: confidence, refuge, expectation, waiting. Some verbs: leaning on, waiting for, looking for, being confident, taking refuge.

Jesus' words at the start of the Passover meal reflect an ardent anticipation: "With desire I have desired to eat this passover with you before I suffer" (Luke 22:15).

The Emmaus disciples expressed their expectation that Jesus was the Messiah. "But we had hoped that He was the one to redeem Israel" (Luke 24:21, RSV). Though suffering a momentary setback, their hope was grounded in fact and revived.

## WHAT IS HOPE?

*Hope Involves Something Good.* After two days in Mexico, a visitor was asked, "Have you been sick yet?" "No," came the answer, "but I hope to." This is a misuse of hope. Hope has been defined as the sweet anticipation of something desirable. We don't hope for a broken leg or a terminal illness. Rather, we hope for good things.

In the New Testament the objects of hope are *always* something good. Of course, what is desired may be good to the wisher's standards and not to the objective biblical morality. For example, Herod was glad when Pilate sent Jesus for interrogation, for "he hoped to have seen some miracle done by Him" (Luke 23:8). The masters of the demon-possessed girl healed by Paul had the apostle arrested because the "hope of their gains was gone" (Acts 16:19). Felix left Paul a prisoner at Caesarea because he "hoped . . . that money should have been given him of Paul, that he might loose him" (24:26).

The Israelites hoped for deliverance from their Egyptian bondage. Abraham hoped for an heir, then later for a suitable bride for him. Ruth gleaned the field of Boaz, hoping for kind treatment from her kinsman.

It is the prospect of something good that leads explorers to months of self-denial, and scientists to countless painstaking experiments. That's why when Soviet troops surrounded Vienna in 1945 the Vienna Philharmonic Orchestra gave a concert, a sort of affirmation that ultimately beauty would triumph over destruction.

*Hope Pertains to the Future.* We speak of hope for tomorrow, never hope for yesterday. Through the Prophet Jeremiah, the Lord links the future and hope as He promises the exiles who wished to return from captivity to their homeland, "For I know the plans I have for you . . . for welfare and not for evil, to give you a future and a hope" (Jer. 29:11, RSV).

The child raised in the ghetto has hope of someday escaping his environment and making a good life for himself out in the world. "Hope that is seen is not hope: for what a man seeth, why doth he yet hope for?" (Rom. 8:24) The opening verse of the great faith chapter says, "Faith is the substance of things hoped for, the evidence of things not seen" (Heb. 11:1).

Wishful thinking is impatient, looking for immediate realization. But true hope requires that "we with patience wait for it" (Rom. 8:25). Because we have been made in the image of God we are able to project our longings into months or years ahead and thus enjoy the anticipation of future good. Augustine said, "Hope deals only with good things, and only those which lie in the future, and which pertain to the man who cherisheth the hope. When hope attains its object, hope ceases to be and becomes possession."

**Theology of Hope**
The theology of hope links hope with man's future in *this* world rather than in the world to come. The theology of hope rests on political theology and social action, perhaps even the use of revolution-oriented solutions, thus earning the name of radical or liberation theology. God reaches toward man from an open future, making possible a new day by changing this present world into a lovely home. It would use the state instead of the church as the key to the future. This hoped-for world seems to depend on man's efforts to bring it in, whereas biblical hope arrives at the new order through the coming again of the Lord Jesus Christ. The theology of hope deals with this world and the here-and-now, whereas Christian hope looks to the future, concentrating its focus of expectancy on the appearance of the King of kings, who will then reorder society and creation.

This does not mean that Christians should neglect concern for the social issues of this life. On the contrary, C.S. Lewis said that a reading of history shows that the believers who did the most for this world were those who thought the most of the next, such as the English Evangelicals who abolished slave trade and child labor. They left their mark on earth because their minds were occupied with heaven. It is as Christians have largely ceased to think of the other world that they have become so ineffective in this. We shall never salvage civilization so long as civilization is our chief object. We must learn to want something beyond even more.

### Guaranteed Hope

*Common* hope is a strong desire or expectation of a future good. But expectations may not be realized. You hope for a good day, but it storms. The farmer hopes for a good harvest, but drought ruins his crop. The sick man hopes for recovery, but doesn't make it. The hungry man hopes for food, but dies of starvation.

Hope in its popular sense often expresses nothing more than a wish based on the law of averages, which often fails to materialize. Dr. Joseph Macaulay in *Devotional Studies in the Epistle to the Hebrews* says, "Hope is a quivering, nervous creature, trying to be bright and cheerful, but alas, very frequently sick abed with nervous prostration and heart failure" (Eerdmans, p. 91).

Up to now we have been speaking of hope in a general way, the expectation of future good which people possess universally. This common hope leads people to believe things will ultimately get better and helps them over the rough spots of life. Now we speak of another kind of hope, a special, superior hope—the Christian hope. Christian hope differs from common hope in several ways. Christian hope belongs only to those who have received Jesus Christ as Saviour, deals more with life after death, and is a guaranteed, assured hope.

Though common hope often expresses nothing more than a desire or longing, Christian hope is different, and must be distinguished from a mere waiting with fingers crossed. Christian hope is always a confident, guaranteed expectation, never carrying the connotation of uncertainty inherent in our cautious English phrase, "I hope so." It was the Christian faith that heightened the meaning of the Greek word for hope, *elipis*. While this was an ambiguous concept in the ancient world, expressing a "hope-so" which might or might not be realized, the Gospel emptied *elipis* of its bleak dubiousness and filled it with certitude and assurance.

Christian hope looks forward to an unconditionally guaranteed glory, where all evil, sorrow, and pain will be forever banished, and an unimaginable inheritance awaits us. Far more than aspiration, hope is a settled conviction, joined to faith and based on God's Word. When Paul said the heathen lived "without hope," he didn't mean that they possessed no aspirations. Rather, in the truest sense, they were without hope because they lived without the definite certitude that comes only from faith in Jesus Christ. Ancient culture at its best had no long-range perspective, but with its cyclic view of history saw man a prisoner from which there was no escape such as the hope of the Second Coming offered Christians.

Hope in the New Testament denotes a joyous expectation of eternal salvation (Acts 23:6; 26:7; Eph. 1:18). The Trinity is involved in our certain hope. The source is our Father—God. "Now the God of hope fill you with all joy and peace in believing, that ye may abound in hope" (Rom. 15:13). Christ, the Son, wrought hope through His cross and empty tomb, so we read, "Christ in you, the hope of glory" (Col. 1:27). Hope is supplied by God's love shed abroad in our hearts by the Holy Spirit, who is also the down payment of our inheritance (Rom. 5:4-5; Eph. 1:14).

The *Pulpit Commentary* says about Galatians 5:5: "What the apostle here calls 'hope' is not the sentiment which we so often thus name when we intend thereby an imperfectly assured

## WHAT IS HOPE?

expectation of some probably coming good. In the apostle's vocabulary it denotes a confident anticipation unclouded by doubt" (Funk & Wagnalls, p. 241). When Paul wrote Titus about the "blessed hope," he was urging him to look forward to the delightful expectation of the "glorious appearing of the great God and our Saviour Jesus Christ" (Titus 2:13).

Hope and assurance are related according to Hebrews 6:11: "And we desire that every one of you do show the same diligence to the full assurance of hope unto the end." Hope, the fruit of assurance, sows a seed in the heart which, in turn, produces more assurance, which produces more hope, and finally results in full confidence. Earthly hopes do not carry assurance, and so may disappoint; but hope based on Scripture is the work of the indwelling Spirit. Thus, hope becomes an anchor for the soul, sure and steadfast (Heb. 7:19).

### Future Beyond the Grave

Man everywhere seems to have a belief in a life that survives death. The late Mrs. Eleanor Roosevelt once wrote, "Almost every person with whom I have ever talked in my world travels has believed in life after death." Tennyson wrote, "If there is no immortality, I shall hurl myself into the sea." Bismarck, a little more restrained, said, "Without hope of an afterlife, this life is not even worth the effort of getting dressed in the morning." Freud called the belief that death is the door to a better life as the "oldest, strongest, and most insistent wish of mankind" (*Newsweek,* Nov. 12, 1965, p. 53).

The pyramids of Egypt were built because of belief in life after death. Each tomb held the items a person's spirit would need on his passage to eternity—furniture, food, weapons, extra clothing, gems, perfumes, makeup kits, and mirrors. Lew Wallace, author of *Ben Hur,* once said, "The monuments of the nations are all protests against nothingness after death; so are statues and inscriptions; so is history."

In his essay on hope, C.S. Lewis says that if we find in ourselves a desire which no experience on this earth can satisfy, then the most probable explanation is that we were made for another world. He speaks of our lifelong nostalgia, our inconsolable longing to be reunited with something in the universe from which we now feel separated, to be on the inside of some door which we have always seen from the outside. Memories are not the real thing itself, but only "the scent of a flower we have not found, the echo of a tune we have not heard, news from a country we have never yet visited."

Because none of the earthly pleasures satisfy this desire does not prove the universe is a fraud, but rather possibly the earthly pleasures were never meant to satisfy it, but only to stimulate it to point us to the real things. Lewis concludes, "I must keep alive in myself the desire for my true country, which I shall not find till after death; I must never let it get snowed under or turned aside; I must make it the main object of life to press on to that other country and to help others to do the same" (*Mere Christianity*, p. 106).

Though many Christian hopes pertain to this life, such as the hope of answered prayer, the hope of another chance after a moral mistake, or the hope of God's providence bringing triumph out of tragedy, most of the Christian hope is wrapped up in the world to come. Contrary to this other-worldly emphasis, many church groups today seem to equate hope with a one-sided emphasis on man's physical, earthly, and economic good. Though important, man's earthly welfare does not take precedence over the welfare of the individual soul and eternal glories. Paul warns, "If in this life only we have hope in Christ, we are of all men most miserable" (1 Cor. 15:19).

Earthly hopes may prove vain, but the resurrection of Jesus Christ launched hope into its high and confident orbit. Peter began his first epistle with a breath of this fresh spirit of

## WHAT IS HOPE?

certainty: "Blessed be the God and Father of our Lord Jesus Christ! By His great mercy we have been born anew to a living hope through the resurrection of Jesus Christ from the dead, and to an inheritance which is imperishable, undefiled, and unfading, kept in heaven for you, who by God's power are guarded through faith for a salvation ready to be revealed in the last time" (1 Peter 1:3-5, RSV).

A few years ago a young man in the metropolitan New York area took a step before his death at 24 which he thought would safeguard his future. Upon his death, Steven arranged to have himself frozen solid until a medical cure was found for the intestinal infection that had made him a chronic invalid.

Steven was a passable poet, photographer, guitarist, a student on the dean's list at New York University, and an avid reader of science fiction. A friend remarked, "He wanted to be in the forefront where science fiction turns into science fact." When Steven's infection stubbornly refused to respond to medical treatment, he followed up an intriguing ad placed in a science-fiction magazine by the Cryonics Society of New York, a movement with the motto, "Never say die!" This society had been founded on the premise that bodies of the "clinically dead" can be put in a deep freeze and later brought back to life.

Seven months before his death, Steven made out a $5 check to join the Cryonics Society. Then he instructed his mother to make sure that once he was pronounced legally dead, his body would be neither buried nor cremated, but frozen. When he died, five members of the Cryonics Society promptly took charge, helping a Long Island funeral director pack Steven's corpse in ice cubes for a two-hour drive to the funeral home. There it was drained of its body fluids, and infused with an "antifreeze" solution to help preserve the body tissues. Then it was packed with dry ice, preparatory to placement in "cryonic suspension" in a "Cryp-Capsule," a giant bottle filled with liquid nitrogen. In that state, Steven will remain indefinitely, maintained at a cost of $200 per year, an expense paid for out of a Cryonics Trust Fund set up by Steven before his death. One magazine titled the story, "Soul on Ice."

His mother said that shortly before his death, Steven made a tape to be placed in the capsule, for he realized he might suffer some brain damage. She commented that his death was easier for her to bear because there wasn't the same finality of putting someone away under the earth. She said, "I had talked about it with Steven, not morbidly, just ordinary conversation, and I came to accept the idea." When asked if she expected Steven to be raised from his Cryonic Capsule, she made this tragically significant comment, "I have only a remote hope for my boy's resurrection."

What a contrast to this remote and unlikely hope is the absolute assurance which the Bible teaches concerning the bodies of those who die trusting in Jesus. Because Jesus Christ conquered death and rose from the grave, He will some day bring back to life all those who have put their faith in Him, giving them perfect bodies, just like His own resurrected, glorified body. "Beloved, now are we the sons of God, and it doth not yet appear what we shall be; but we know that, when He shall appear, we shall be like Him; for we shall see Him as He is" (1 John 3:2).

# ❧ THREE ❧
# WHERE DO WE GO FOR <u>HOPE</u>?

A TV Special told the moving story of Brian Piccolo, star halfback on the Chicago Bears football team, who died at 29 in 1970. His wife, Joy, recalled how hard her husband fought to make the team and to develop his abilities in order to make a lot of money and be happy. Brian became successful. They enjoyed the money he made. But Joy lamented later, "I saw him young and dying, and there wasn't any answer. By then the money could have bought most anything, but it couldn't bring back Brian. There has to be an answer somewhere."

Where do people go for hope?

### Hope Is Inherent in Man
People everywhere seem to possess hope. Jerry Ballard, Executive Director of World Relief which has brought over 40,000 refugees to the U.S., says the common thread that enables a person to endure oppression in his own country, risk storms and piracy on makeshift craft on the high seas, make it through the rigors of a refugee camp and ultimately to America is the

hope of survival. How do you keep going when you see your wife and daughter raped before your eyes, your baby die in your arms, and yourself thrown overboard near some desolate island? As long as you believe there's a way out, there's hope. Ultimate poverty is the poverty of hopelessness.

Hope is a part of God's image in man, a gift of God's common grace. Just as God is good in sending sunshine and refreshing rain on the evil as well as on the good, in giving outstanding talents to the non-Christian, in granting happy marriages to the unsaved, in restraining evil in the world through governments so that unbelievers as well as believers may enjoy a measure of peace, so in common grace God grants hope to all people so that man may not despair. Much of human enterprise is the result of creative hopefulness, including the nurture of our children, our works of art and other esthetic endeavors, the construction of buildings, and the institution of government. Without this common stimulus of hope we would not make progress.

In her book, *On Death and Dying* (Macmillan), Elisabeth Kubler-Ross asserts that the one thing that usually persists through all the five different stages of dying is hope. Even her most realistic patients left the possibility for some last-minute intervention or discovery of some miracle drug. All her patients maintained a little bit of hope even in the most difficult times. She observed that when a patient stopped expressing hope, it was usually a sign of imminent death.

Many of our Proverbs, poems, and sayings reflect the commonness of hope.

Cicero gave us the well-known, "While there's life, there's hope."

Thomas Carlyle asserted, "Man is, properly speaking, based upon hope; he has no other possession but hope."

Alexander Pope reminded us, "Hope springs eternal in the human breast."

# WHERE DO WE GO FOR HOPE?

William Shakespeare declared, "The miserable have no other medicine but only hope."

Samuel Johnson put it, "It is necessary to hope, though hope should always be deluded; for hope itself is happiness, and its frustrations, however frequent, are yet less dreadful than its extinction."

## Natural Hope Is Weak

Many hopes are based on flimsy foundations, and can shatter in a hundred pieces. The shipwrecked sailor who imagined a tender reunion with loved ones may at last die of exposure on the vast ocean expanse. The prisoner who hoped for acquittal may receive a stiff sentence. The terminally ill patient who hopes for some miraculous cure may die in a few weeks. A student foolishly longs for an A on a test for which he did not study. Hope may stand on imaginary ground, grasp at impossibilities, feed on bubbles, and end in despair. Hope without a solid basis is like a cloud without rain. Says the Hindu proverb, "There is no disease like hope."

Another factor which reveals the anemic nature of natural hope is its limited outlook. So many of our goals are temporal and short-ranged. A high-schooler can hardly wait for June and graduation. The excited college-age girl hopes her steady boyfriend will soon pop the question and marry her. The college senior hopes for a good job offer. The newlyweds hope for healthy children, a lovely home, financial security, and happiness.

But short-range hopes provide motivation only until we stop to ponder. Why bother to keep body and soul together, get an education, marry, and struggle for success in the business world, establish a home and raise children, if all these are to be eventually torn away from us and buried in the dust of a smashed universe?

Common hope looks in the wrong places for strength. Some hopes in which men have trusted from time to time only to find them false are: dwellings (Job 18:14); idols (Ps. 115); princes (Ps. 146:3); riches (Prov. 11:28); nations like Ethiopia and Egypt (Isa. 20:5); horses (Isa. 30:16); armies (Isa. 31:1-3); and men (Jer. 17:5).

### God—Our Ultimate Source of Hope

Asks the psalmist, "Why art thou cast down, O my soul? And why art thou disquieted within me? Hope thou in God" (Ps. 42:5). Repeatedly the psalmist enjoins us to hope in God (71:5; 131:3; 146:5). The prophet asks, "Are there any among the false gods of the nations that can bring rain? Or can the heavens give showers? Art Thou not He, O Lord our God? We set our hope on Thee" (Jer. 14:22, RSV). Jeremiah affirms, "Blessed is the man that trusteth in the Lord, and whose hope the Lord is" (17:7).

The New Testament likewise declares unequivocally that God is our hope. "Now the God of hope fill you with all joy and peace in believing" (Rom. 15:13). Paul links Jesus Christ with the Father as the source of hope: "God our Saviour, and Lord Jesus Christ, which is our hope" (1 Tim. 1:1). Hope is futile, flimsy, and false unless reposed in an omnipotent, faithful, and loving Lord.

Dr. Joseph Macaulay in his *Devotional Studies in the Epistle to the Hebrews* says, "Natural hope is the next-door neighbor to despair, only they are on bad terms. Christian hope is poles apart from despair, has no fellowship with it. Even in the days of calamity, Christian hope has nothing to despair of. While the man in the flesh is apt to say with Jacob, 'All these things are against me,' Christian hope teaches us to say, 'For our light affliction, which is but for a moment, worketh for us a far more exceeding and eternal weight of glory' " (Eerdmans, pp. 91-92).

# WHERE DO WE GO FOR HOPE?

Natural hope is anemic because it has nothing solid to feed on. But Christian hope is based on the promises of God, guaranteed by the resurrection of Christ, and appropriated by faith.

### Grounded in Gospel Promises

Psalm 119, which extols the Word of God in practically every one of its 176 verses, refers frequently to the hope which the Word engenders. For example, "Remember the Word unto Thy servant, upon which Thou hast caused me to hope" (v. 49; also see vv. 43, 114). Elsewhere the psalmist says, "In His Word do I hope" (Ps. 130:5).

However, the main promises which give hope are those that point to the finished, redemptive work of Christ through the cross and the empty grave. Because He bore the penalty of our sins at Calvary, He has broken the barrier which keeps us from fellowship with God. The righteousness of Jesus Christ is imputed to us, making us accepted in the beloved Son. God now regards us as completely righteous. Our hope is found in the Gospel of God's grace. The Heidelberg Catechism, over 400 years old, puts it this way:

> *Question:* What is your only comfort in life and in death?
>
> *Answer:* That I belong—body and soul, in life and in death—not to myself, but to my faithful Saviour, Jesus Christ, who at the cost of His own blood has fully paid for all my sins.

Our first parents, exiled from Eden, were given the gift of hope through the promise of a Redeemer, often called the Protoevangelium (Gen. 3:15). This hope was fulfilled in Christ. Our hope centers in the majestic work of God in the life, death, and resurrection of Jesus Christ. We now look forward with hope because we can look backward to Christ's redemptive work. In Him we have forgiveness and eternal life. He is called "the hope" (Col. 1:27).

God makes our hope doubly sure. He does so by supporting the revelation of His message with an oath, "that by two immutable things, in which it was impossible for God to lie, we might have a strong consolation" (Heb. 6:18). If God's promise is as dependable as His oath, why did God have to resort to an oath? Not to make His Word more sure, but to make us more assured. Knowing our frame and tendency to doubt, He did that which was utterly unnecessary to Himself. Thus, we who have fled to Him for refuge can "lay hold upon the hope set before us; which hope we have as an anchor of the soul, both sure and steadfast" (6:18-19). With the hymn writer we say:

> My hope is built on nothing less
> Than Jesus' blood and righteousness;
> I dare not trust the sweetest frame,
> But wholly lean on Jesus' name.

### Guaranteed by the Resurrection

Peter says that God has given us "a living hope through the resurrection of Jesus Christ from the dead" (1 Peter 1:3, RSV). What a stupendous truth that He who was crucified and buried came out of the grave on the third day, victor over death and conqueror of the tomb! Some who find it difficult to believe in a literal resurrection say that His spirit rose, but not His body. Those who accept the Resurrection only in a spiritual sense really mean that the body remained in the tomb. Yet the biblical record reports an empty tomb.

Many attempts have been made by unbelievers to account for an empty tomb. A survey of these leading theories along with their evident difficulties should strengthen our faith in the bodily resurrection of Christ. Peter exhorts us to "be ready always to give an answer to every man that asketh a reason of the hope that is in you with meekness and fear" (1 Peter 3:15). Ours is a reasonable hope.

*The swoon theory* suggests that Jesus didn't die, but merely fainted. Revived by the damp sepulchral air, He pushed His way out and appeared to His disciples who thought He had risen from the dead. However, Roman soldiers, so experienced in the gruesome task of crucifying, would not have been so easily deceived and would have known when a victim had expired. Official government pronouncement, after investigation by Pilate's representatives, declared Jesus deceased. The women came early the first day of the week to perform ministrations on a corpse, not on a man in a coma. How could a person who had swooned, severely weakened by unimaginable agony and lack of food and drink, ever push back a stone which normally took several muscular men to move? In such a state of physical suffering, how could our Lord walk several miles to Emmaus, appearing not as a wounded weakling, but with majestic deportment?

*The wrong tomb theory* says the disciples went to the wrong sepulcher. But loved ones usually find the grave of a relative with little difficulty, even with rows of graves in the vicinity. How could His followers have been mistaken when this was likely the only sepulcher in Joseph's garden? If it were the wrong tomb, why did every group go to the wrong tomb? How did the angel know they were going to the wrong tomb and to which wrong tomb? How did the graveclothes land in the wrong tomb?

*The subjective vision theory* claims that, in their excitement over the possibility of Christ's return from the dead, the kindled imaginations of the disciples fancied they saw Him. Psyched to expect Him back, they suffered hallucinations. But this does not jibe with the facts. How could such visions develop when they did not expect Him to rise? How could the same inward vision come to several persons simultaneously?

The disciples doubted that we might believe.

*The objective vision theory,* also called the telegraph theory, developed by a Canon of the Church of England, holds that God miraculously sent the disciples an objective vision of the risen Christ to motivate them to Gospel preaching. But God would never promote His work by trickery. Since this theory requires supernatural intervention, why not accept the miracle of the Resurrection?

*The theft theory* assumes that someone stole the body. But who would steal it? Certainly the Jews would not—for that was exactly what they did not wish to happen. Because they recalled Jesus' saying that He would rise after three days, they petitioned Pilate for guards to make the tomb secure till the third day, "lest His disciples come by night, and steal Him away, and say unto the people, 'He is risen from the dead' " (Matt. 27:63-64).

Nor did the guards steal the corpse. Their job was to guard it. Their excuse sounded lame: "His disciples came by night, and stole Him away while we slept" (Matt. 28:13). How ridiculous their testimony would have sounded in court—"While our eyes were closed in sleep, we saw His disciples come and steal His body."

*The falsehood theory* is really part of the *theft theory* for it holds that the disciples stole the body, then preached His resurrection. This would characterize these witnesses as not merely mistaken, but false. This assumption makes all the apostles unmitigated liars. The superstructure of nineteen centuries of Christian preaching has then been based on flimsy fabrication. The perpetrators of such willful imposture should be considered knaves, not honored apostles.

Psychologically, how can we explain the sudden change in the apostles from cowardice to courage? In Gethsemane, they forsook Jesus and fled, and Peter cowered before a maid. About two months later Peter stood before thousands, fearlessly flinging the charge, "Him . . . ye have taken, and by wicked hands have crucified and slain" (Acts 2:23). Only their firm conviction in the resurrection of Christ can account for the willingness of the apostles to bravely suffer beatings, imprisonment, and martyrdoms which ended most of their lives. They had seen One who had conquered death, and because He lived, they too would live, no matter what happened to them.

I have a book whose foreword tells how two men of acknowledged talents determined to expose the Bible as an imposture. Their strategy was to attack two bulwarks of Christianity: the resurrection of Christ and the conversion of Paul. These men lived in the 18th century and moved on intimate terms with Alexander Pope, Philip Chesterfield, and Dr. Samuel Johnson. Neither had read to any extent in the New Testament, so in fairness to their assignment, they examined the biblical evidence, though they were much prejudiced. As a result, both men were converted. They gave us two of the most valuable treatises in favor of the Bible, one entitled *Observations on the Resurrection of Christ* by Gilbert West, and the other whose foreword tells this story, *Observations on the Conversion of St. Paul* by Lord Lyttleton (American Tract Society, New York).

In 1984 our Christian magazines reported on a book by Pinchas Lapide, an orthodox Jewish scholar who specializes in the New Testament. In the book, *The Resurrection of Jesus: A Jewish Perspective* (Augsburg), he argues for the resurrection of Jesus as a historical fact. Lapide says, "I have written that God raised Jesus from the dead because I'm thoroughly convinced it's true." Strangely though, he denies that Jesus was the divine Son of God or the long-expected Messiah of the Jews.

The Resurrection proves Jesus to be all He claimed. He is "declared with power to be the Son of God by His resurrection from the dead: Jesus Christ our Lord" (Rom. 1:4, NIV). The Resurrection shows He is victor over death. He let His body become a corpse and be buried, but He emerged from the grave. He who reinhabited His crucified corpse pealed out, "I am He that liveth, and was dead; and behold, I am alive forevermore, amen; and have the keys of hell and of death" (Rev. 1:18). His resurrection guarantees the resurrection of all the dead at some future time, plus the sure fulfillment of all aspects of the believer's hope.

## Appropriated by Faith

Without the deep assurance of faith, true hope could not exist. Though faith and hope are inseparably connected, and sometimes used interchangeably, yet despite their affinity, faith is faith, and hope is hope. There are some differences.

*Faith is the root; hope is the fruit.* Faith produces hope. Romans 5 begins with the believer "justified by faith," then rejoicing "in hope of the glory of God" (5:1-2). Romans 8 starts with the Christian under no condemnation, then proceeds to the glowing expectancy of a redeemed universe and our own individual hope (8:1, 19-25). God has promised His children full deliverance from sin and complete enjoyment of Himself. Paul wrote, "For we through the Spirit wait for the hope of righteousness by faith" (Gal. 5:5).

Faith is basic. Hope issues from and is fed by faith. Ambrose, fourth century Bishop of Milan, said, "The heir must believe his title to an estate before he can hope for it; faith believes its title to glory, and then hope waits for it. Did not faith feed the lamp of hope with oil, it would soon die" (*Pulpit Commentary* on Hebrews 11:1). Hope has been called faith on tiptoe.

*Faith is directed toward the Promiser; hope looks toward the things promised.* Faith focuses on *whom* we trust, whereas hope zeros in on *what* we anticipate will be ours someday. Faith has for its primary object God the Father and His Son, while hope has to do with the content of faith, which is the glory of our future inheritance. Faith assures us that God cannot lie, whereas hope confidently anticipates the promises He will most certainly keep.

*Faith relates more to the past; hope looks ahead to the future.* Faith has a major dimension in the past. Of course, our faith exists at the present time, but points back to a historical event when Christ entered this space-time universe and "suffered under Pontius Pilate, was crucified, dead, and buried . . . the third day He rose again from the dead." Our faith also involves an act of committal at some past point when we rested our confidence in the Gospel, namely the death, burial, and resurrection of Christ (1 Cor. 15:3-4). Though our faith will continue into the future, it is nevertheless rooted in the past.

But hope deals with the future. The Nicene Creed points up this difference between faith and hope. It ends: "I *believe* in one universal and apostolic church . . . and I *look for* the resurrection of the dead, and the life of the world to come." Though we look for the resurrection (and all involved in the Christian's inheritance) with solid assurance, we still look for it. When hope can grasp its object, it is no longer hope (Rom. 8:24).

Faith is something we have now. Hope is something whose content is yet to be realized. As *The Living Bible* translates Hebrews 11:1-2, faith "is the confident assurance that something we want is going to happen. It is the certainty that what we hope for is waiting for us, even though we cannot see it up ahead."

## The Triad—Faith, Hope, and Love
Hope is closely allied with faith and love as important elements of the Christian life, though not always in the same order (Rom. 5:1-5; Gal. 5:5-6; Col. 1:4-5; 1 Peter 1:3-8, 21-22). Paul wrote the Thessalonians that he remembered "without ceasing your work of faith, and labor of love, and patience of hope in

our Lord Jesus Christ" (1 Thes. 1:3). Perhaps hope was last because it was the chief need of their church at this time, as they faced their current tribulations.

The best known Bible reference that includes all three is the last verse in the great love chapter. "And now these three remain: faith, hope and love. But the greatest of these is love" (1 Cor. 13:13, NIV). Love is the greatest because it existed from eternity past, making possible the redemption in which we put our faith. God's love also makes possible the good things for which we hope. When faith has turned to sight, and hope to fulfillment, love will still flow on. Faith may produce hope, but love is the first and final thing. Note that this verse doesn't say that God is faith, or God is hope, but it *does* say God is love.

The God of the universe sent His Son to be my Saviour. Where I spend eternity depends on my relationship to Jesus Christ. When I repent of my sins and confess Him as my Saviour, a light flashes through the murk of my earthly pilgrimage, dispelling the gloom of hopelessness. The Christian faith, not some flimsy, short-range goal, provides hope for man's highest health.

# FOUR
# THE BELIEVER'S GUARANTEED HOPE

DR. JAMES DOBSON reports on the death of a fellow doctor who, after a quarter of a century on the university medical faculty, had earned the admiration of both professionals and patients for his wide medical knowledge and research findings. This doctor had reached the pinnacle of success in his field, tasting fame, money, and status.

At the first staff meeting after the funeral, a five-minute eulogy was read by a colleague. Then the chairman asked the entire staff to stand for a minute of silence in memory of their deceased co-worker. Dobson began to wonder, *Lord, is this what it all comes down to? We sweat and worry and work to achieve a place in life and to impress our fellowmen with our competence. Then finally, even for the cleverest among us, all these experiences fade into history as our lives are summarized with a five-minute eulogy and sixty seconds of silence. It hardly seems worth the effort, Lord.*

Dobson was also struck with the collective inability of that faculty to handle the questions raised by their colleague's death. *Where has he gone? Will he live again? Will we see him on the other side? Why was he born? Were his deeds observed by a loving God? Is that God interested in me? Is there meaning beyond professorships, successful research, and expensive homes and automobiles?* The silence of those 250 highly trained physicians shouted their inadequacy to cope with these issues. "Then," says Dobson, "a wave of relief spread over me as I thought of the Bible's teaching on this topic" (James Dobson, *Straight Talk to Men and Their Wives,* Word Books, pp. 201-202).

Though secular thinking regards hope as mere sentiment or wishful thinking, the Christian's hope is settled, sure, certain, and focuses on an inheritance that can never fail. It is guaranteed to last forever. Just what is the good that is assured and secured for the believer in the world to come?

## Our Inheritance in General

For the Old Testament Israelite, an inheritance was a portion of land allotted each tribe to be possessed and enjoyed. However, the New Testament believer's inheritance is not physical or earthly, but spiritual and heavenly. Paul refers to our inheritance as our unseen hope for which we wait with patience (Rom. 8:25). He writes of the hope to which we've been called (Eph. 1:18); the hope laid up for us in heaven (Col. 1:5); our glorious hope (2 Cor. 3:11-12); our good hope (2 Thes. 2:16); and the hope of eternal life (Titus 3:7). The author of Hebrews speaks of the hope set before us (Heb. 6:18). Peter, the apostle of hope, describes this hope as living, suggesting energy and vibrancy (1 Peter 1:3, NIV).

Though the word *hope* occurs in Paul's epistles around forty times, we search in vain for any full or detailed explanation. His phrase *hope of glory* has been singled out as the most satisfactory, yet least explainable description (Col. 1:27). The New Testament offers few answers to many of the questions we wish to ask about the nature of life after death, probably because such knowledge is beyond our finite comprehension. Much that is stated in Revelation about the heavenly Jerusalem is expressed in negative terms—no tears, no pain, no sorrow, no night, no crying, no death (Rev. 21:4, 25).

The believer's hope includes:
- enjoyment of the presence of Christ (Ps. 16:11; Phil. 1:23)
- eternal rest in a heavenly home (Rev. 14:13)
- suffering ended, tears wiped away, and death destroyed (Rev. 21:4)
- reunion with loved ones (1 Thes. 4:16-17)
- completion of our salvation with conformity to the image of Christ (Rom. 8:29-30)
- the wonders of heaven (John 14:2)
- the resurrection with a perfect body (Phil. 3:21)
- abundant entrance into heaven (2 Peter 1:11)
- the Lord's approval, "Well done." (Matt. 25:21)
- treasure in heaven (1 Cor. 3:8)
- reigning with Christ in a position of responsibility (Rev. 20:4)

*Enjoying the presence of Christ.* To the dying thief Jesus promised, "Today shalt thou be with Me in paradise" (Luke 23:43). Just before his martyrdom, Stephen saw the heavens open and the Son of man standing on the right hand of God. As pelting rocks crushed out his life, he exclaimed, "Lord Jesus, receive my spirit," then passed into the presence of Christ (Acts 7:59). Paul taught that to be absent from the body was to be present with the Lord (2 Cor. 5:8). Thus, when on trial before Nero, Paul knew that execution would usher him immediately into the presence of the Lord.

What a day when we see Jesus! The veil will be lifted, and the panorama of His glory will be revealed, as will the nailprints in His hands and feet. Perhaps this is the crowning satisfaction of heaven, enjoying the presence, not only of the Son but also of the Father and Holy Spirit, growing in knowledge and drinking at the living fountains of water. This coming communion with God has been called "the beatific vision." How radically different is this hope from the colorless expectation of absorption into the universe, or nirvana with its extinction of desire and loss of individual consciousness.

*Completion of salvation—conformity to the image of Christ.* Bishop Taylor Smith, once chaplain-in-chief of the British Armed Forces, was asked by a young, zealous stranger, "Are you saved?" The Bishop replied, "I am in the process of being saved." The youth thought the Bishop's view deficient, whereupon the Bishop explained the three tenses of salvation. In the past at *regeneration,* the believer *has been* saved from the penalty of sin. Now, in the present, the growing believer *is being* saved from the power of sin through the process of *sanctification.* Some future day the believer *will be* made complete in the divine image and saved from the very presence of sin, resulting in the perfection of *glorification.*

Though we grow toward maturity in our Christian experience, it will always be partial maturity in this life. At our glorification in the world to come, our incomplete maturity will give way to the fullness of perfection. The believer's glorification is repeatedly mentioned in the New Testament (Rom. 8:30; 2 Thes. 2:14; 2 Tim. 2:10; Heb. 2:10; 1 Peter 5:10; 2 Peter 1:3). In this life we rightfully hope to receive divine grace, guidance, provision, and spiritual help for our daily walk and warfare. But only in heaven will we be assured of perfect righteousness. In that day we shall be without moral blemish (Eph. 5:27); faultless before God's presence (Jude 24); holy (Col. 1:22); without offense (Phil. 1:10); blameless (1 Thes. 5:23); and conformed to the image of Jesus Christ (Rom. 8:29). Though we are now being changed into Christ's image, the final transformation will not occur until Christ comes (1 John 3:2).

## THE BELIEVER'S GUARANTEED HOPE

*The wonders of heaven.* Heaven is a real place, not the figment of our imagination nor the projection of our wishes. Jesus said, "In My Father's house are many mansions; if it were not so, I would have told you. I go to prepare a place for you" (John 14:2).

Man's redeemed soul requires a renewed environment. The Bible begins with a righteous, unfallen man in a perfect setting and ends with glorified man in Paradise and his archenemy, Satan, cast into the bottomless pit. In this remade heaven and earth exist no famine of food or water, no hospitals, no cemeteries, no rent, no mortgage payment, no tax, no utility bills, and no darkness—for the Lamb Himself is the light (Rev. 21:23).

*A delightful place.* The lovely sights, sounds, and sensations of this life are but a poor foretaste of the wonders of heaven. Unimaginable color, beauty, and symphony await us. Scott Carpenter, the second American to circle the earth in space, said, "The colors glowed vigorously alive with light." He told how he watched a sunset narrow "until nothing was left but a rim of blue." He termed the experience all but supernatural. It has been suggested that a taste of the delicious fruits of heaven will make the nicest fruits of earth taste like medicine.

Going from here to there will be like going from a dungeon to a palace, or like a soldier, surviving on K-rations in some far-off battlefield suddenly transferred to his mother's Thanksgiving dinner with turkey, pumpkin pie, and all the trimmings.

*A busy place.* Will eternity be a perpetual afternoon siesta, as we recline on flowery beds of ease? Or will we be lounging on cloud nine, strumming away on our harps? No, ecstatic worship, thrilling tasks, and fantastic people will eliminate boredom and depression, and make for the abundant life. "In Thy presence is fullness of joy; at Thy right hand there are pleasures forevermore" (Ps. 16:11).

*Music and worship.* Heavenly music will surpass anything

here on earth. Hearing the "Hallelujah Chorus" sends chills up and down the spines of many saints. Imagine the emotional impact when heaven's vast and magnificent choir peals out its choral numbers over all the starry space. Naturally, worship will focus on the One on the throne and the Lamb beside Him (Rev. 5:13).

*Work and rest.* In addition to worshiping the Lord with music, we shall learn in heaven. We will never come to know everything, for omniscience belongs only to God. Yet in heaven we will have an insatiable desire and almost limitless ability to learn (1 Cor. 13:12). In this life the greatest scholar can learn only so much about his particular field. Up there, we shall be able to delve into as many fields and as deeply as we wish.

God's servants shall serve Him day and night (Rev. 7:15). In heaven we will be assigned dominion over some territory; we will co-reign with the Lord (Rev. 20:4). Exactly how isn't revealed, but doubtless it will be commensurate with our gifts and interests.

How do we reconcile work in heaven when it's supposed to be a land of eternal rest? The concepts of labor and rest are combined in heaven as we serve Christ without frustration and weariness of toil. Our service will be a sort of pleasurable, restful labor.

*Fellowship.* Present will be the redeemed of all ages. Saints from Bible times will be there, along with characters from church history like Augustine, Luther, Livingstone, Calvin, Spurgeon, and D.L. Moody. We shall meet the martyrs of every century, including those who most recently laid down their lives under Communist tyranny.

Our loved ones in Christ will be there. We shall know each other, just as Moses and Elijah recognized each other on the Mount of Transfiguration, though separated by 500 years of history (Luke 9:30-31). If fellowship is meaningful on earth, how much more so it will be in heaven, when we are surrounded by people who share our devotion to Jesus Christ.

A father and son had been shipwrecked. Together they clung to a piece of floating debris until the son was washed off and vanished from the father's sight. The father was rescued unconscious the next morning. Hours later, he awoke in a fisherman's hut. He was lying in a warm, soft bed. In heartbroken agony, he remembered his son. His last memory was of his boy swept off the piece of debris, vanishing out of sight. But as he turned his head in the fisherman's hut, he saw his boy resting in the other bed across the room. His heart leaped for joy.

One by one, followers of the Lord are carried away by the billows of time. But some day, awakening in resurrection splendor, all God's family shall be together again in the land where our love shall be forever perfect, and our joy forever full.

*A perfect body.* Man's glorified soul living in a renewed environment will require a perfect body. Part of our hope is a powerful and incorruptible body, fashioned like Christ's resurrected body. Paradoxically, our raised bodies will be both similar and dissimilar to our earthly bodies. Using the analogy of sown seed, Paul points out that what springs up is the same grain as the seed sown, and yet is different in its full-grown form. Likewise, our new bodies will have continuity and identity with our present bodies, so that we will recognize each other in heaven. But our new bodies will be different from our present ones because they will be powerful, glorious, imperishable and immortal (1 Cor. 15:35-43).

In his defense before Governor Felix, Paul spoke of "hope toward God . . . that there shall be a resurrection of the dead" (Acts 24:15). He spoke of groaning within ourselves "waiting for the adoption, to wit, the redemption of our body" (Rom. 8:23). He also affirmed that "if our earthly house of this tabernacle were dissolved, we have a building of God, an house not made with hands, eternal in the heavens. For in this we groan, earnestly desiring to be clothed upon with our house which is from heaven" (2 Cor. 5:1-2).

Afflictions here are but momentary compared with the eternity of glory awaiting us there (Rom. 8:18). Paul calls it "a far more exceeding and eternal weight of glory" (2 Cor. 4:17).

*Reward in heaven.* Though salvation is a gift and cannot be merited, rewards are prizes earned through the quality of our service. The Bible warns against losing "those things which we have wrought," urging us onward so "that we receive a full reward" (2 John 8). The New Testament speaks of crowns. Paul wrote of a test by fire to determine whether our works were gold, silver, precious stones, or wood, hay, and stubble. If our works last through the fire, we shall receive a reward. If not, though saved, we shall suffer loss (1 Cor. 3:11-15).

Jesus taught that persevering believers would hear, "Well done, thou good and faithful servant; thou hast been faithful over a few things, I will make thee ruler over many things" (Matt. 25:21). Our position of responsibility in eternity will be commensurate with the degree of our faithfulness in this life. Whatever form our rewards assume, they constitute the Lord's recognition of human effort on His behalf.

Jesus said, "Lay up for yourselves treasures in heaven" (Matt. 6:20). How do we make deposits in the bank of heaven? By our consistent, daily, godly living, good deeds done in Jesus' name, use of our talents and gifts to build up the body of Christ, giving of money to help the deprived and hungry, supporting Bible-teaching churches, Christian colleges, Gospel-spreading missionaries and other evangelical organizations, by our witness and outreach, and by our care for the needy.

Back when foreign exchange regulations prevented my father, up in Canada, from sending money down to the U.S. to make purchases, he would write me, "Son, if you will use some of your money down there to order that item mailed to me, when you come up to Canada on your next trip, I'll have the money waiting for you." Similarly, our Heavenly Father says,

"My child, if you will take some of your money and use it for My work on earth, when you come up to heaven some day, I'll have it waiting in your account in the bank of heaven."

A man gave several thousand dollars to help build a church. Then came the 1929 crash. He lost everything. Someone said, "If you had that money you gave to start the church, you would've had enough to set yourself up in business again." He replied, "I would have lost that money too in the crash. As it is, it's the only money I saved. It's now in the bank of heaven yielding interest which will accumulate until eternity. Hundreds have come to Christ through the church it helped build."

Jesus said, "Make to yourselves friends of the mammon of unrighteousness; that, when ye fail, they may receive you into everlasting habitations" (Luke 16:9).


The Permanence of Our Inheritance
A few years ago a resident of Connecticut died leaving a large estate, including one foreign account, a deposit over $26,000 in the Royal Bank of Canada in Toronto. Succession duties owed the Dominion of Canada government came to over $3,000. Province of Ontario taxes came to nearly $11,000. Cost of probate was slightly over $1,000, so that $15,000 stayed in Canada and $11,000 was returned to Connecticut. Then over here, U.S. federal and Connecticut taxes amounted to more than $14,000. Not only did the combined taxation of both countries wipe out the original bank account of $26,000, but it required an additional $3,000 to be paid out of the rest of the estate.

This could never happen to the Christian's inheritance. Peter uses four qualities to describe the permanence of our inheritance: incorruptible, undefiled, unfading, and reserved in heaven (1 Peter 1:4).

*Incorruptible.* Unlike apples, clothes, or trees, it will not

spoil. Nor can enemies ravage it.
*Undefiled.* It will not rust nor stain.
*Unfading.* It does not dissipate nor disappear.
*Reserved in heaven.* It is preserved, guarded, protected, beyond reach of decay, thieves, bank failure, disaster, and death. Our inheritance is safe in the holiest region of God's creation, "where neither moth nor rust doth corrupt, and where thieves do not break through nor steal" (Matt. 6:20).

### Inheritance for Whom?
Peter declared this inheritance was reserved for them who had been begotten again unto a living hope (1 Peter 1:3). It is for those born again into God's family and thus made heirs of God and joint-heirs with Jesus Christ.

Not only is the inheritance reserved, but likewise believers "by God's power are guarded through faith for a salvation ready to be revealed in the last time" (1 Peter 1:5, RSV). What good is an inheritance if the heirs never receive it? But believers will receive their inheritance, for the heirs of salvation are kept for the inheritance, even as the inheritance is reserved for them.

Our hope is linked with our eternal home. We are just pilgrims and strangers down here. *Home* conjures up all sorts of memories and pleasantries. When a psychology class visited a mental hospital, a patient, handsome, personable, dressed up in suit and tie, and hair neatly combed, excitedly told the students, "I'm going home tomorrow!" The class was happy for him until a doctor whispered, "He tells everyone that. He's been going home tomorrow for 17 years now." We need the same anticipation about going some day to our heavenly home, a hope which is not mistaken.

Dr. Harry Rimmer, well-known Bible teacher a generation ago, wrote the following message to Dr. Charles Fuller, speaker on the Old Fashioned Gospel broadcast:

## THE BELIEVER'S GUARANTEED HOPE

Next Sunday you are to talk on heaven. I am interested in that land because I have held a clear title to a bit of property there for over 55 years. I did not buy it. It was given to me without money and without price. But the Donor purchased it for me at a tremendous sacrifice. I am not holding it for speculation since the title is not transferable. It is not a vacant lot. For more than half a century I have been sending material out of which the greatest architect and builder of the universe has been building a home for me which will never need to be repaired because it will suit me perfectly, individually, and will never grow old.

Termites can never undermine its foundation. Fire cannot destroy it. Floods cannot wash it away. No locks or bolts will ever be placed upon its doors.

There is a valley of deep shadows between the place where I live and that to which I shall journey. I cannot reach my home in that City of God without passing through that dark valley of shadow. But I am not afraid. He has stuck by me through thick and thin since we first became acquainted.

I hope to hear your sermon on heaven next Sunday, but I have no assurance that I will be able to do so. I may not be here while you are talking next Sunday evening, but I shall meet you there someday.

Harry Rimmer's hope of living another week on earth was without certainty, but his ownership of an eternal home in heaven was part of his guaranteed Christian hope.

# FIVE
# THE THERAPY OF HOPE

A FAMOUS AMERICAN cardiologist said in his autobiography, "Hope is the medicine I use more than any other. Hope can cure nearly everything" (Dr. R. McNair Wilson, *Doctor's Progress*, Erye & Spottiswoode, p. 250). Another doctor commented, "If you lead a person to believe there's no hope, you drive another nail in his coffin."

Dr. Armand May Nicholi II says, "Psychiatrists have long suspected that hope fosters health, both physical and emotional. An increasing body of medical evidence documents the deleterious effect that depression and hopelessness have on physical health." He quotes Freud who as early as 1905 declared that "duration of life can be appreciably shortened by depressive effects" ("Why Can't I Deal with Depression?" *Christianity Today,* November 11, 1983).

In an experiment at the University of Rochester School of Medicine, 54 patients awaiting open-heart surgery were interviewed before their operations. Significantly, 80 percent of those who died after surgery had been depressed.

For years scientists have found clues that hopelessness often sets the spadework for the development of organic disease. Dr. Hans Selye, pioneer in the field of stress, said, "When people truly want to live, they make a greater effort and their immunization system somehow works better" (*Modern Maturity,* October-November, 1978, pp. 9-10).

### Hope and Survival

Dr. Harold G. Wolff, Professor at Cornell University Medical College, reported that of 6,000 U.S. prisoners of war captured by North Korea, about one-third died. Doctors on the scene observed that the cause of death in many cases was a vague sort of "give-up-itis." Depressed, a prisoner would become lethargic, refuse to eat or drink, stare into space, and finally die. Reports from Vietnamese POW camps revealed the same pattern. But in camps where discipline and purpose kept the spark of hope alive, the survival rate was much higher.

Dr. Wolff also studied several World War II prison camp survivors who later became strongly effective citizens. They viewed their incarceration, though painful, as but a temporary interruption; they focused on life as it would continue after their release with job, marriage, and family. They even cultivated new interests. One man raised rabbits for food. Others organized academic courses among themselves, teaching and holding seminars. Though after liberation some had short-term illnesses, their vitality seemed undiminished. Some went on to major responsibilities. The lesson flashes clear—hope is medicinal. When hope dies, man dies (Dr. Harold G. Wolff, "What Hope Does for Man," *Saturday Review,* January 5, 1957).

### Hope Enhances Mental Health

A tough, young marine-prisoner, promised release by the camp commandant if he cooperated, survived two years in relatively good health. But when it dawned on the marine that his captors had no intention of releasing him, he rejected food, became a zombie, and in a few weeks died. A psychologist analyzed, "He was sustained by hope of release. When he gave up hope, believing all his efforts would continue to fail, he died." "Hope deferred maketh the heart sick" (Prov. 13:12).

In contrast, Corrie ten Boom in a German death camp felt the sting of a lash, saw people marched to the gas chambers, and saw her sister die. Philip Yancey in *Where Is God When It Hurts?* writes, "There is another element in *The Hiding Place,* an element which has proved almost untenable to secular reviews of the subsequent movie—the element of hope and victory. Woven through *The Hiding Place* are threads of small miracles, Bible studies, hymn-sings, acts of compassion and sacrifice. And throughout, Corrie and her sister Betsie continue to trust in a God who sees them and cares" (Zondervan, p. 93).

Psychologists tell us that for highest mental health, a person needs hope. Without the sustaining vision of some definite achievable and abiding goal, one cannot be well integrated. Samuel Coleridge put it:

> Work without hope draws water in a sieve,
> And hope without an object cannot live.

A ward in a state hospital had 88 patients, 51 of which had been bedfast for ten years. Forty-one were spoon-fed every meal. The average stay for these hopeless, bedridden, vegetating patients was ten years.

But then the method of treatment was changed. The patients were given individual attention, music, TV, a cage of canaries, lovely curtains, birthday parties, meaningful work like painting the shuffleboard court on the floor, and handcrafts. At the end of a year, only nine of the surviving 83 were still bedfast. Twelve had gone home (six to live alone), five had died, and four were gainfully employed and self-supporting.

## THE THERAPY OF HOPE

Former Minnesota governor Albert H. Quie wrote, "If there is one central approach to life that determines its quality and direction it is found in the opposite attitudes of hope and despair. When people see their situation as hopeful they attack the day's tasks with a light heart. When there is no 'light at the end of the tunnel' then even the simplest of tasks become overwhelming" (Prayer Breakfast Leadership Letter, November 1983).

### Hope Sustains in Trials

A Lutheran pastor was imprisoned at Dachau concentration camp with little likelihood of ever coming out alive. In the one monthly letter allowed him, his wife chatted about the family and her love for him, then at the bottom printed Acts 4:26-29. Looking up the reference, he found the verses part of a speech by Peter after his release from jail:

> The kings of the earth stood up, and the rulers were gathered together against the Lord, and against His Christ. For of a truth against Thy holy child Jesus, whom Thou hast anointed, both Herod, and Pontius Pilate, with the Gentiles, and the people of Israel, were gathered together, for to do whatsoever Thy hand and Thy counsel determined before to be done. And now, Lord, behold their threatenings: and grant unto Thy servants, that with all boldness they may speak Thy Word.

That afternoon the pastor was called to face interrogation. Waiting his turn, he saw the door open. A fellow minister coming out slipped something into his pocket. The interrogation went well. Back in his bunk, the pastor reached in his pocket to see what the other minister had slipped there. It was a matchbox, minus matches but with a folded paper on which was neatly printed Acts 4:26-29. No way could his wife and this minister have known each other. This text about the victory of Christ revived his hope, enabling him to bear the rest of his incarceration with the greatest peace. Years later, he became a guide at Dachau and related his testimony to thousands of tourists.

One result of justification is a triumph based on hope and victorious over tribulation (Rom. 5:1-3). The successful endurance of tribulation in turn reinforces our hope (vv. 3-5). This strengthened hope helps us persevere in later afflictions. Paul wrote of the "patience of hope" (1 Thes. 1:3). The heart that possesses hope will persist through the trying situations that intervene between the present sufferings and the future realization of that hope. Hope knows that all things will be better by and by. Waiting may be tough and aggravating, but eventually relief will come. Confident expectation that "joy cometh in the morning" will help us plod through the night (Ps. 30:5).

Our helmet to protect against the sharp blows of life is "the hope of salvation" (1 Thes. 5:8). Hebrew believers who had already endured "a great fight of afflictions" were exhorted to lay hold on the hope set before them, for it was "an anchor of the soul, both sure and steadfast" (Heb. 10:32; 6:18-19). When exposed to danger, our anchor, not connected to the ocean below but to heaven above, will help us ride out the storm, give us renewed buoyancy, and keep us from vacillating midst the blowing winds of false doctrine. Peter calls it a living, vibrant hope because of the resurrection of Christ from the dead (1 Peter 1:3). Because He lives, we can face tomorrow.

The message of Christian hope, propounded regularly from pulpits and sung meaningfully by congregations, has undoubtedly kept untold thousands of fragile people on an even keel instead of going under midst the tempests of life. Hope helps us maintain our sanity in an otherwise unfriendly and inexplicable universe.

# THE THERAPY OF HOPE

## Bill Mulhall

Bill Mulhall, a young man with a long-term diabetic condition, often attended our church in Nanuet, New York. Diagnosed diabetic in his childhood and frequently ill because of complications, Bill hopefully plugged along. He graduated from The Kings College, and earned a master's degree in science from Rutgers. Then he served on the faculties of three New York area colleges, and married a lovely Christian nurse. In 1979 Bill's condition worsened. Contemplating going on the kidney-dialysis machine, his hope revived when he received a kidney transplant at Columbia Presbyterian Hospital in New York City. Complications followed. Bill's vision became foggy. The transplant developed a fungus growth. Strong medicine left him with unpleasant side effects. Eventually Bill recovered sufficiently to resume part of his teaching load and fill preaching engagements in local churches. Then in mid-October 1983, just after he and his wife had completed the recording of their first professional Gospel album, Bill passed away from cardiac arrest.

Ten days before his death, Bill addressed a symposium of doctors at Columbia Presbyterian Hospital on the subject of *Renal Transplantation and Hope*. He said, "I was uplifted by the hope which the initial treatment plan presented to me. In order for hope to be an actuality in a person's life, it must have its roots in fact, not fiction. False hope is worse than no hope, for in the end, unrealistic hope not only leaves the patient with no hope, but also with disappointment and depression."

Midway through his presentation Bill said, "I think that this would be an opportune moment to clearly establish the integral link between faith and hope." He then quoted Hebrews 11:1, "Now faith is the assurance of things hoped for, the conviction of things not seen" (RSV). Relating this verse to his situation, he explained, "The comfort of faith and hope given me by my nephrologist at the first meeting increased and substantiated the hope already present within me. Furthermore, I believe, beyond any shadow of a doubt, that the circumstances which gave me hope and faith, were orchestrated by my Lord."

To keep the doctors from thinking he had "gotten religion" because of his serious illness, Bill said, "The events of my declining health had not been the motivation which turned me to God. Twenty-four years earlier (before the transplant) at the age of four, I had asked Jesus Christ to come into my heart as my Saviour and Lord, to forgive me of my sins and guide my life. This decision in no way assured me of a life of ease, wealth, and freedom from pain. However, I did find that in whatever situation I found myself, my Lord was there with me. This provided continuous strengthening of my faith, giving me the assurance that there was not going to be any experience in my life, where I could not place my faith and hope in Him, and not be disappointed, no matter how dark the path! It has been my personal experience that faith in God can be compared to a skeletal muscle; the more it is used, the stronger it becomes, and the stronger the hope it evokes and sustains."

The purpose of his presentation, he stated, was his fervent "wish to create an awareness of how essential it is to continuously evoke and nurture hope, and perpetuate it in the renal transplant patients." Bill concluded with a personal testimony, "I found that my faith and hope in God, combined with positive, optimistic, hopeful attitudes of my physicians, gave me the intangible, yet all too real component . . . hope."

Interestingly, for the last six years of his life, Bill served as Telephone Minister of Hope-Line, a telephone counseling service sponsored by Tele-Missions International. Day and night, hours on end, after teaching his college classes, Bill conversed with distressed youth, drug addicts, and suicide-prone people. He who seemingly had so little to hope about radiated hope to the hopeless, some of whom, as a result, have attended our church.

Three days after Bill's presentation, the leader of the symposium wrote Bill's wife that her husband's outlook was an unforgettable example of how life can maintain qualities of fulfillment even when confronted by obstacles that appear to be overwhelming.

## Biblical Examples

When Abraham was around 75, and Sarah 65, God promised they would at some time have a baby (Gen. 12:1-4). Years passed. When he was 99 the Lord appeared to Abraham to inform him that about a year later his wife would have a son. Listening at the tent door, Sarah laughed. It was impossible! Abraham and Sarah were to call the boy Isaac, which means *laughter* in Hebrew (17:19). God would have the last laugh as He kept His word (21:1-5).

Though outwardly laughing, inwardly Abraham believed God. "Against all hope, Abraham in hope believed and so became the father of many nations, just as it had been said to him" (Rom. 4:18, NIV). We should learn that when the answer never seems to come, or things don't seem to add up, hope should help us to hang in there tough.

Because of his dreams of someday ruling over others, Joseph was able to withstand years of adversity. Sold as a slave into Egypt (Gen. 37:27-36), hope doubtless helped stabilize his life. Joseph served Potiphar so well he became his master's deputy over all the household (39:1-6). Later, falsely accused by Potiphar's wife, hope again gave him motivation to do his dungeon duty faithfully, so that again he was put in charge of the other prisoners (vv. 7-23). Though he may not have realized the vast extent of his coming power as second-in-command of all Egypt, hope of future leadership spurred Joseph to patient endurance of affliction.

Called to lead the Israelites out of Egypt's bondage, hope

sustained Moses through the many dark days when Pharaoh not only refused to let the Israelites go, but increased their work load as well. But God had promised, so Moses kept hoping. Finally came the day when the Israelites marched safely through the Red Sea which then engulfed the pursuing Egyptian army (Ex. 3:7—14:31).

Virtually in the middle of the five chapters of the Lamentations of Jeremiah over the desolation of his nation, the weeping prophet thought of the faithfulness and goodness of God. Then he wrote, "This I recall to my mind, therefore have I hope. . . . The Lord is my portion . . . therefore will I hope in Him" (Lam. 3:21, 24).

Confined to his Roman hired-house prison when he so desperately wanted to preach the Gospel unhampered, Paul didn't moan about his situation (Acts 28:16-31). Rather, he rejoiced in his sufferings for he saw how through them the Gospel made great advance. Some of his guards, likely members of the crack Praetorium unit, became believers in the Gospel (Phil. 4:22) which they carried right into Nero's palace. Runaway slave Onesimus was converted. Christians were stirred by Paul's example to witness with greater boldness. And Paul was able to write four letters now in the sacred canon: Ephesians, Philippians, Colossians, and Philemon. Motivating his endurance was his earnest hope. "According to my earnest expectation and my hope, that in nothing I shall be ashamed, but that with all boldness, as always, so now also Christ shall be magnified in my body, whether it be by life, or by death" (Phil. 1:20).

When the believers of Asia Minor were passing through the furnace of torture, banishment, and martyrdom, the Holy Spirit inspired John, himself a prisoner on the Isle of Patmos, to write the Book of Revelation. This volume portrays the glorious coming of the conquering Christ to put down His enemies, vindicate His own, and reign as King of kings and Lord of lords.

## THE THERAPY OF HOPE

### Hope Gives Peace at Death

Armand Mayo Nicholi II begins his *Christianity Today* article, "Why Can't I Deal with Depression?" by pointing out the indelible impact on the world made by Karl Marx and Sigmund Freud. Then he reminds us that both men led a strong attack on the Christian faith, with Marx calling religion the "opiate of the people" and Freud defining God as the projection of a child's wish for a protecting, powerful father. Finally, Nicholi recalls that both died bitter and disillusioned men, virtually friendless, without inner peace and overwhelmed with despair and hopelessness. They had no spiritual resources to help them.

At the end of his article, Nicholi contasts Marx and Freud with C.S. Lewis, who embraced the Christian faith and used his talents to influence people in a noble direction. Then he describes how Lewis reacted to the loss of his wife. He did go through all the processes of grief, but later emerged from his sorrow with renewed strength and unspeakable joy derived from Him on whom his hope was grounded. Unlike Marx and Freud, Lewis had resources to see him through.

What do folks do who have no Christian hope at the time of death? They are of all men most miserable (1 Cor. 15:19). A few years ago the Canadian ambassador to Egypt, a distinguished diplomat and ranking scholar on Japanese culture, committed suicide. In his suit pocket was a scrawled note, "I have no option. I kill myself because I live without hope."

How different from those who rest their hope in Christ. A busy doctor overworked himself into a fatal illness. His widow, a Christian, deeply in love with him, bore up heroically during the funeral. Her friends thought she would break down when grief set in. But to their amazement, her spirits continued buoyant. One day while visiting her, they blurted out, "What's your secret? How have you remained so peaceful?"

"Come with me to the doctor's waiting room," she answered.

## THE SUSTAINING POWER OF HOPE

Leading them down the hall to his reception room, she snapped on the light. All stood in silence until someone pointed to a sign hanging on the office doorknob. Then they understood. The widow related, "The maid forgot to remove that sign. She put all the other rooms in order, but perhaps the Lord let her leave it here. Right after his death, I spotted the hand-lettered sign, hanging a little unevenly, just as he had left it. That message gave me the courage to go on."

The sign read, *Gone for a little while. Will be with you soon.*

Hope for tomorrow gives strength for today.

# SIX
## DASHED HOPES

You Can't Judge a War by isolated battles. When all England waited for the result of the Battle of Waterloo, word came, flashed by signals across the English Channel: *Wellington defeated.* Then thick fog set in. Despair enveloped England. Later, when the fog lifted, two more words were signaled. The complete message read: *Wellington defeated the enemy.*

A Chinese parable tells of an old man who lived with his son in an abandoned fort. One night the old man's only horse wandered away. His neighbors came to say how sorry they were about his misfortune. He replied, "How do you know this is ill fortune?"

A week later the horse returned bringing a whole herd of wild horses with it. The neighbors helped capture the wild horses, congratulating the man on his newly acquired good fortune. The old man smiled. "How do you know this is good fortune?"

One day the man's son, riding one of the wild horses, was thrown and ended up with a crippled leg. The neighbors appeared again to commiserate on his bad luck. The old man asked, "How do you know that it is bad luck?"

The story ends here, though likely it could go on more. Sorrow and heartache, though painful at the time, often turn out to be a blessing somewhere down the road. God knows the end from the beginning. The Christian can trust divine providence.

J.B. Phillips paraphrases Romans 8:28-29: "We know that to those who love God, who are called according to His plan, everything that happens fits into a pattern for good. For God, in His foreknowledge, chose them to bear the family likeness of His Son." Dashed hopes are included in God's design to help promote the believer's spiritual growth.

It may take a while to see how a particular tragedy fits into the pattern. When Winston Churchill lost a British election in the 1940s, his wife said it was a blessing in disguise. He replied, "If it's a blessing, it's well disguised." Sometimes the disguise comes off fairly soon. In other cases, the disguise may take months or years to fall off. And in many instances, we must wait till we reach heaven to ask the Lord to explain why.

### Quick Explanations

The lone survivor of a shipwreck, finding himself on an uninhabited island, soon managed to build a shelter where he stored food and a few items collected around the island. Every day he scanned the horizon for a passing ship. One day he spotted a boat, ran to the shore, and waved frantically. But the boat moved steadily away till it became a speck on the horizon. With hope of rescue dashed he returned to his hut, only to find it in flames. Doubly disappointed, he sat down in despair. The next day a ship arrived. The captain explained, "We saw your smoke signal!"

Mary and Martha could not understand why Jesus didn't come immediately to heal their brother Lazarus. When He did arrive, they each lamented separately, "Lord, if Thou hadst been here, my brother had not died" (John 11:21, 32). But they were soon to learn why He had not intervened. It was to show His power over death as He performed the mightiest miracle of His ministry, the raising of Lazarus after four days in the grave. Explanation of why Jesus failed to respond to their first call for help came to Mary and Martha within a few days.

The first Easter afternoon two followers of Jesus were walking the road to Emmaus with heavy hearts. Their hopes had been dashed. As they discussed the events of the past few days, a stranger joined them, seemingly ignorant of those happenings. Surprised how anyone living around Jerusalem could not have heard, they told Him about the mighty prophet from Galilee whom they hoped would have redeemed Israel. They spoke of His crucifixion and rumors that He was alive. At this point the stranger reproved them for their failure to understand that the prophets taught that the Messiah would both suffer and enter His glory. Later in their home, in the familiar breaking of bread, He revealed Himself to them. Though tired, they hurried back to Jerusalem to join the other disciples behind closed doors, and report their glorious experience (Luke 24:13-31, 33-35). Within three days, their dashed hopes had been explained.

Toward the end of World War II a young sailor, fresh from the Pacific conflict and with limited furlough time, rejoiced when he was allotted a seat on a military C-46 out of Alameda Airport headed for Chicago where his girlfriend lived. Gliding through the gateway into the 21-seat plane, he buckled his safety belt and relaxed. The right propeller churned the air, then the left. The chocks were pulled from under the wheels. The plane was about to taxi for the takeoff. Suddenly outside was the stationmaster, wildly waving his arms. Behind him a vice-admiral waddled under the weight of two huge duffle bags. "Hold that flight," hollered the stationmaster.

The sailor's heart sank. When the door opened, he heard

three names, one of which was his. The three were told to get off the plane while the vice-admiral and his two bags took the three seats. Sitting dejectedly on the ground as the plane took off, the sailor looked up, "God, why did You let this happen to me? You know I want to get home!"

Happily, three hours later the sailor caught another plane for Chicago. That evening as the plane descended toward the Kansas City airport for a brief stop, huge searchlights flared all around. "Turn out those lights," shouted the pilot over his radio system. "We don't need them to land."

"Identify yourself," replied the tower. "Which flight are you?" The pilot identified his plane.

"Where's the flight that left Alameda three hours before you? It hasn't come in yet."

The flight never did come in. Its wreckage was found in the Rockies some days later. Today, that sailor is a well-known radio announcer, Bob Murfin, who emcees the morning commuter-hour program over Chicago's Moody radio station, WMBI.

### Delayed Explanations

A young widow named Ruth turned sobbingly from a fresh grave. Numb with sorrow, she shuffled falteringly toward home. Her mother-in-law, Naomi, decided to return to her homeland of Israel. Ruth went with her. Little did Ruth realize that there she would meet a prosperous and godly man who would redeem her inheritance, marry her, and share his home with her. How could she know that she would be blessed with a child, become an ancestress of the promised Messiah, receive mention in Matthew's genealogy, and have a book of the Bible named after her? Hope had dissipated when her husband died. But the providence of God revealed the reason why a few years later (Ruth 1:3-19; 2:2-9; 4:1-17; Matt. 1:5).

# DASHED HOPES

Perhaps no greater tragedy could have hit the early church than the stoning of its staunch deacon, Stephen. Yet that seeming disaster led to the conversion of the church's most zealous persecutor. From that stoning flowed much of the rest of the Book of Acts, chapters highlighting Paul's three missionary journeys, arrest at Jerusalem, detention at Caesarea, and voyage to Rome. Someone thinking of Stephen's non-vengeful martyrdom, remarked, "Had not Stephen prayed, Paul would not have preached." It took several years before it became evident how God had overruled the wrath of man in the stoning of Stephen by the great missionary endeavors of Paul, who was somewhat responsible for that stoning (Acts 6—7; 9:1-31).

In violation of an English law, John Bunyan planned to preach to a gathering in a farmhouse. Approaching the meeting place after a day's work as a mender of pots and pans, this uneducated, simple saint was informed he would be arrested if he proceeded to preach. Walking in the woods to think it over, he decided to go on with the service. Arrested, he spent the next twelve years, except for an interval of a few months, in Bedford jail. How low his hope must have been, but from that little cell he wrote the immortal allegory, *Pilgrim's Progress*, still unrivaled three centuries later.

Years ago a tornado struck the prairies of Minnesota, injuring hundreds and almost demolishing the town of Rochester. A doctor and his sons worked for days, bandaging wounds and setting broken limbs. Their heroic work did not go unnoticed. Financial backing was offered for a large hospital provided the doctor and his two sons took charge. They agreed, opening in 1889 a clinic which soon attracted wide attention. People have since come from all walks of life for treatment at the Mayo Brothers Clinic.

How tragic the news thirty years ago that five young American missionaries had been killed by Auca Indians in the Ecuadorian jungle. But since then this area has opened up to missionaries, all the killers of the martyred missionaries have embraced the Christian faith, and hundreds have volunteered for missionary service.

In the summer of 1967 Joni Eareckson had a diving accident that completely changed her life. When it dawned on her after months of treatment that she would always be paralyzed, she was devastated. Her whole life would be radically different—no more sports cars, horse shows, perhaps no more dates. She found herself alone, a paralyzed body between two sheets. Strapped to a canvas bed, facing down, she saw hot tears drip to the floor. For months she was consumed with questions about God. It took a long time for her to accept her condition.

Today thousands have been blessed by Joni, a popular, inspirational speaker at banquets and conventions. She's appeared on the "Today" show and in *People* magazine. Her artwork graces cards and stationery in stores nationwide. She is now married, drives a van, and is engaged in a ministry of helping the handicapped. She had hoped. . . . But she came to see that God had other ways through which to provide her an abundant life.

**Heaven's Explanations**
In some cases explanation of our blasted hopes may show up in a few weeks or in several years. But in many other cases, we won't know the answer till we reach heaven's shore and let the Master Planner explain.

Even when a partial answer comes in this life, we may have to wait till eternity to get the full story. In Joni's situation some of the mystery has cleared, but many unanswered questions remain. At the end of the *Joni* film she says, in effect, "I don't know why, but I know who has the answer. And I can wait."

In this life Job never did find a satisfactory reason for his sufferings. When he came to see that God was completely

## DASHED HOPES

sovereign, able to do whatever He wished and without explanation, then it was that he abhorred himself, and repented in dust and ashes. When we read the story we are aware of information denied Job, namely the dialogue in which Satan slanders Job before God by claiming he was pious because he was prosperous. Job did not know that God permitted Satan to afflict him to show the devil that Job would glorify God even in adversity. The eyes of heavenly spectators watched as Job championed God's honor. Yet Job had no idea he was in the arena representing the Lord, and probably never knew till he arrived in heaven.

When God seems not to hear our cry for help in times of affliction, our pain intensifies. Scripture tells of people delivered from trouble. Television programs contain testimonies of healings, yet our bodies are wracked with pain, and loved ones linger with terminal illness. When heaven is silent, we must remember that all events can be viewed from two angles—from our viewpoint and from God's.

When a Sunday School bus was hit by a train at a railroad crossing, killing two children, the preacher sent a telegram to relatives living at a distance: "God is too wise to make a mistake, and too kind to be cruel." If we change the first letter of *d*isappointment, we get *H*is appointment, which hints that the thwarting of my purpose may be God's better plan for me, even though it comes in a disguise it will wear till eternity.

A woman's life was ebbing away in a current of severe pain. Her son, bending over her, said, "Mother, I can't understand why God should let you suffer so." Calmly she whispered two stanzas of a hymn:

> Blind unbelief is sure to err,
> And scan His work in vain;
> God is His own interpreter,
> And He will make it plain.

## THE SUSTAINING POWER OF HOPE

> God's help is always sure,
> His methods seldom guessed;
> Delay will make our pleasures pure,
> Surprise will give it zest.

*The Living Bible* translates Proverbs 20:24: "Since the Lord is directing our steps, why try to understand everything that happens along the way?"

# SEVEN
# HOPE OF A SECOND CHANCE

SOME YEARS AGO I was standing at the front of a Kansas church after delivering the evening sermon. A middle-aged man greeted me with these words, "When I was a young man, I felt the call of God to be a missionary, but I turned my back on His call. I've been successful in my work, but there's an emptiness in my heart." Turning away, he solemnly added, "Wherever you go, warn young people not to say no to God's will."

Did that man have to spend the remaining years of his life with that disturbing thought gnawing away at his spirit?

A deacon gets involved with a lady in the church choir. The affair is exposed. Both parties genuinely repent. Is there hope that their marriages can be salvaged, and both people still prove useful in Christian service?

A trusted employee embezzles sizeable company monies for his personal use. An audit catches up with his chicanery. Though he is fired, he is mercifully spared prosecution when he promises restitution. Will he ever find another job in the financial world? Is a second chance possible?

According to counselors, multitudes are hurting because

they think that once they have committed some dishonest, foolish, even immoral deed, they are forever consigned to some second-rate limbo of spiritual uselessness. They feel that an egg once broken, like Humpty Dumpty, can never be put back together again. They lament, "Once I've been sidetracked, I'm a failure. My spiritual effectiveness is ended."

We're not talking about another chance for salvation after death, for the Bible rules out such a second chance. "It is appointed unto men once to die, but after this judgment" (Heb. 9:27). In His goodness, God gives countless opportunities to receive Christ in this life, but none after death.

**Episode of a Second Chance**
When Don Baker was pastor of the thriving Hinson Memorial Baptist Church in Portland, Oregon, he received a long-distance phone call that shattered his day. A long-time friend told him that a Hinson staff member had been involved in immorality in other places where he had ministered, and that the story was beginning to surface. A stunned Baker put the phone down, laid his head on his desk, and cried.

The staff member, a dear friend and colleague of Baker's, was admired by the entire church as hard-working, poised, capable, and professional. What should be done? The details of this church's dealings with a sinning brother are told in Baker's book, *Beyond Forgiveness—The Healing Touch of Church Discipline* (Multnomah). Instead of sending him quietly away or dismissing him publicly or blowing the whistle on him so as to make all future ministry impossible, Baker initiated a process of church discipline which he hoped would lead to the minister's ultimate restoration in God's service.

First, Baker confronted the staff member, who immediately admitted his indiscretions. The staff member agreed to confess the whole matter to his wife, and did so in the presence of

## HOPE OF A SECOND CHANCE

Baker. To Baker's relief and surprise, the man's wife responded with immediate forgiveness.

Baker reported all this to the members of the church board, who called a church meeting the very next Sunday night to discuss it with the congregation. Immediately after the regular Sunday evening service, Baker kindly, gently, and tactfully explained the situation. He gave biblical reasons why the matter should be handled openly, and called on the staff member, who with great humility, much weeping, and loss of control at times, confessed his indiscretions.

Then Baker outlined the recommendations of the board, to which the staff member had already agreed. This minister was to surrender his ordination papers until he was again qualified for the ministry, not engage in public ministry without the board's permission, submit to extensive psychological counseling, remain at Hinson so that members could help in his restoration, and seek secular employment.

The staff member kept all the conditions, even though he didn't do too well on his secular job, saw his wife become seriously ill, and lost his home. A year after the church meeting both the minister's psychologist and his wife declared him a new man. He was re-ordained and told he could accept any offer of church service. Though none came for a while, two years from the Sunday night of his public humiliation a call came from a church which he accepted.

Comments Baker, "The counselor had given him two things he desperately needed: hope and acceptance" (*Beyond Forgiveness—The Healing Touch of Church Discipline,* Multnomah, p. 90).

### The God of the Second Chance
Our God has the ability to bring good out of evil. He can show His favor despite a fiasco. Without all the king's horses and all

the king's men, He *can* put Humpty Dumpty together again.

*Abraham.* God told Abraham to leave Ur of the Chaldees and travel to a promised land (Acts 7:2-4). But halfway there, a long distance from Canaan, Abraham settled down in Haran, a city perhaps similar to his native Ur. Was it the feebleness of his father or fear of unknown territory that caused Abraham's incomplete obedience? However, God's word came a second time to leave country and kindred for "a land that I will show thee" (Gen. 12:1). Abraham's full obedience, after a second start, has brought blessing to the world through his descendants who gave us the knowledge of God, the Word of God, the church of God, and the Saviour.

*Moses.* Moses possessed some knowledge of his call to lead his people out of the bondage of Egypt, but he acted precipitously when one day he killed an Egyptian, supposing that "his brethren would have understood how that God by His hand would deliver them" (Acts 7:25). Forced to flee to Midian, Moses lived in a desert for forty years, perhaps thinking his assignment to liberate his fellow-Israelites was canceled. But when he was eighty years old, God spoke to him from a burning bush: "Come now therefore, and I will send thee unto Pharaoh, that thou mayest bring forth My people . . . out of Egypt" (Ex. 3:10). God gave Moses a second chance. Even though Moses offered excuses, the Lord continued to deal kindly with him.

*The Israelites.* How many chances God gave His people! When the Israelites, possessors of the Promised Land, disobeyed His Law, He let neighboring nations nip off a piece of Israel's territory. When they repented, He gave them another chance, sending a judge to rally them to victory over that enemy. This happened over and over. The Book of Judges can be represented by a down/up cycle. The downside would picture their decline and defeat. At the bottom came their cry of repentance. Then the upswing would indicate deliverance by a judge from the hand of their enemy. The top of the cycle would

## HOPE OF A SECOND CHANCE

signal their walk with God (Jud. 2:16-19; 3:9, 15; 4:3; 6:6; 10:10-16).

How often we fail in the Christian life. But just as often, God gives us another opportunity. Over and over He grants forgiveness and restoration. Says the hymn, "He giveth, and giveth, and giveth again."

*Jonah.* One of the most hopeful verses in the Bible is Jonah 3:1: "The word of the Lord came unto Jonah the second time." God's word had come to Jonah the first time to go to Nineveh, "that great city, and cry against it" (Jonah 1:1-2). But Jonah deliberately disobeyed. Instead of heading east 500 miles toward Nineveh, he paid passage on a boat going west 2,000 miles to Tarshish, the end of the known world. God prepared a great fish to bring the prophet back, which swallowed, preserved, and then ejected him near home territory (1:3-17; 2:10).

Could we blame God if He had then put Jonah on the shelf? Hadn't Jonah disqualified himself from ever again serving as a prophet to proclaim God's message? Even had Jonah repented, wouldn't God have been justified in benching him from further service?

But disobedience to God doesn't automatically bar us from later usefulness. God's commission came a second time to Jonah. Obedience this time issued in one of the largest mass conversions in history, the entire population of Nineveh. If, like Jonah, we have messed up by running away from God, He will give us a second chance.

*David, Peter, Mark.* David committed the double sin of adultery with Bathsheba and arrangement of the death of her husband, Uriah, in battle. David testified in his psalm of penitence that not only would the joy of salvation be restored to him, but that a renewed commission would enable him to teach transgressors the divine way (Ps. 51:10, 13).

How Peter needed another chance after so shamefully denying Jesus three times, especially after his boast that he would die before denying the Lord. Not only did Peter weep bitterly when Jesus gazed at him at the crowing of the cock, but he must have shed acid tears repeatedly in those interim hours before the private interview with Jesus on the resurrection day (1 Cor. 15:5). Later at a breakfast by Galilee Jesus publicly commissioned Peter to feed His sheep (John 21:1-19). What a power Peter became!

But Peter needed still another chance. Later, at Antioch, he departed from the Gospel of pure grace by refusal to eat with Gentile (uncircumcised) believers. Boldly confronted by Paul, Peter saw the error of his way and returned to the purity of 100 percent grace (Gal. 2:11-14). Surely Christ who spoke of forgiving 70 times 7 would grant His stumbling, bumbling followers several chances (Matt. 18:22).

John Mark, helper to Paul and Barnabas on the first missionary journey, defected along the way. From Asia Minor, perhaps to escape the hardships he saw coming, he returned to Jerusalem. Though Paul refused to take him on his second journey, gracious Barnabas gave him a second chance (Acts 12:25; 15:36-39). Even though he had flunked his first major assignment, Mark was later welcomed back by Paul who found him profitable for the ministry (2 Tim. 4:11). Mark also wrote the second book in the New Testament.

Jeremiah, watching a potter at work, saw the whirling wheel and the directing hand that fashioned vessel after vessel. Then something happened. A handful of clay with some hidden mixture of foreign substance foiled the potter. The potter stopped the rotating wheel, crumbled the misshapen vessel with his fingers, remedied the defect, and restarted the wheel. Under his direction, the marred lump of clay grew into a beautiful receptacle (Jer. 18:1-4).

We should dispossess ourselves of the mistaken notion that if we turn away from God's will we are forever thrown on the ash heap. Satan likes to muddle us into thinking that we are beyond salvage, doomed to God's second best. God never discards a repentant life. Restoration qualifies for renewed service. No matter what the sin, God can forgive and reshape the life. Marital infidelity and divorce are not unpardonable sins, necessarily assigning a person to the discard pile the rest of life. Most churches would not let David nor Solomon near their pulpits today, yet their writings are in the inspired Bible, and their names inscribed right in the middle of Christ's genealogy in Matthew.

### Decide to Do God's Bidding

G.K. Chesterton said, "There is a proverb, 'As you have made your bed, so you must lie in it,' which is simply a lie. If I have made my bed uncomfortable, please God, I will make it again."

When we fall, we pick ourselves up and get moving once more. Similarly, if we take a moral tumble, we should not despair nor panic, but repent and say, "The game is not over yet. I will follow God's will from here on." By doing His will from then on, what we thought was second-rate can become God's first-best. Some use their former disobedience as an excuse to do nothing. Others are genuinely paralyzed into inactivity. But we shouldn't quit. The highest, first, and best will of God is that duty right at hand. He can use a clean vessel today. Whatever would please God now, regardless of my previous mistakes, is God's best for me.

Jerry met and married Pat after coming home from the Navy. Four sons were born in a few years. Jerry devoted his time to making a good living in the insurance business. But he never wore his wedding ring, telling Pat he didn't want to get it caught on the lawn mower or any other piece of equipment. He paid little attention to his sons' school and sports activities. Pat attended Little League games, scout meetings, and church.

Suddenly, it seemed to Jerry as if all his friends, including his wife and four boys, became zealous Christians. He ridiculed them, took up transcendental meditation, flying lessons, and golf. They were patient with him. One day the Lord spoke to Jerry and turned his life around. He began going to church, making new friends, meeting with Christian businessmen, and attending a men's Bible study group.

Later at a wedding, Jerry saw his marriage commitment in a new light. He realized that Pat had given him 25 years of her life, and he had never even worn his wedding ring. Going home, he found the ring and wore it from then on.

Trying to recall his own wedding, Jerry couldn't remember what vows he and Pat had made because he had arrived with a terrible hangover. He had never even bought Pat an engagement ring—she had paid for her own. Visiting a jeweler-friend, Jerry bought a beautiful set of both engagement and wedding rings. Then one night he asked Pat, "Ever thought of remarrying?" Puzzled, she thought Jerry was asking for a divorce. Then he brought out the ring set, told her he had not been the greatest husband, but that he loved her. He asked for her forgiveness and suggested they renew their vows. Then he slipped the rings on her finger.

Jerry and Pat were married a second time in the quiet of their pastor's study with just the immediate family present. All went to dinner after the ceremony. Looking around the table, Jerry realized it was the first time they had been together in a public place since the boys were small. Assuming his role as Christian head of a Christian family, he said grace. Opening his eyes he saw his mother-in-law beaming from ear to ear. He knew his "second" marriage was off to a good start.

What about Consequences?
Though the Lord may give us another chance, we may have to suffer some consequences. David, who disrupted a family

## HOPE OF A SECOND CHANCE

through adultery and murder, reaped a harvest of similar trouble in his own family. Jonah discovered, according to divine geometry, that a detour is the roughest distance between two points. A young man who damaged himself permanently on drugs had to settle for limited Christian service. A young lady who married an unbeliever found herself in a nagging situation in which her husband not only constantly ridiculed the Christian faith, but also hassled her every time she or the children tried to go to church.

On the other hand, God may overrule our mistakes for His glory, making the wrath of men to praise Him. Tourists watched a group of Persian weavers making beautiful rugs, their fingers moving skillfully under the direction of a master weaver in charge of seeing that the design was faithfully carried out. Asked what happened if one of the weavers made a mistake by using a wrong color or wrong stroke of the shuttle, the master weaver replied that usually the weaver did not have to take out the wrong color or stroke, but simply wove the mistake into his pattern. God is able to overrule our blemishes for His glory. Where sin abounds, divine grace does much more abound.

Augustine said that by making stepping stones out of our past sins we may rise to heights of maturity. Had we not fallen, we would be unaware of our weaknesses. Also those who have recovered from a fall may be able to keep others from erring, or point out the way of restoration. Jesus told Peter, "When thou art converted, strengthen thy brethren" (Luke 22:32).

A prison chaplain tells how in his mid-twenties he took a trip from California through southern Oregon in a worn-out Plymouth. The highest speed he could coax from the groaning engine was 35 miles per hour. On the third day of the trip in a severe storm that dropped visibility to near zero, the engine sputtered and died. Coasting to the side of the road, he realized he was 30 miles from the nearest town, and nightfall was near.

## THE SUSTAINING POWER OF HOPE

Suddenly, a vehicle approached—the only car he had seen in several hours. As it stopped behind him, he was apprehensive. A tall man, barely visible, came to the driver's window. The driver rolled down the window and shouted above the storm, "The engine died."

The stranger moved to the front of the car and raised the hood. Striving to keep his balance against the force of the wind, he reached in, adjusted something, then signaled the driver to turn on the ignition. To the driver's amazement, the engine sputtered and turned over. In gratitude the driver shouted, "I was afraid the engine had failed for the last time."

Then the stranger hollered back, "Every car has at least one more start in it if given the proper attention." Suddenly, the wind subsided and the rain diminished to a drizzle. Softly the stranger continued, "The same principle applies to people. Someday you will have occasion to apply this knowledge. Remember that as long as a single spark remains, it's not too late either for a car or a human being to make a fresh start."

Twenty-five years later the driver came to appreciate the significance of those words. About to begin as a chaplain in a major prison, he noted the hopeless expressions on the faces of most of the inmates. His mind bridged the quarter century as he again heard those words, "As long as a single spark remains, it's not too late either for a car or a human being to make a fresh start."

The person who has the slightest urge to get back on God's track, even though off it for years, can have a new start. There *is* a land of beginning again.

# EIGHT
# HOPE IN THE FACE OF DEATH

A Boy Living in Idaho could never forget a lumber buyer named Benham who stayed a week in his home. An outspoken atheist, Benham could repeat persuasively the major arguments of agnostic Robert G. Ingersoll. He stated openly that he spent most of his money and time proving God did not exist. Irrevocably he held there was no afterlife, no heaven, and no hell.

Twenty years later the boy, grown to manhood, was attending a convention in St. Paul, Minnesota, when he noticed a familiar gentleman. It was Mr. Benham, who also recalled the youth and invited him to lunch. It was soon evident that the atheist had lost his poise. He acted like a man facing a death sentence.

Now 71, Benham explained that he had an incurable blood disease, and less than half a year to live. He then launched into an incident about an elderly lady who lay at death's door in a local hospital where Benham had gone for a check-up. While there, he had been enlisted by a nurse sent out by the dying woman to get three witnesses to a deathbed will she could not sign because of a paralyzed arm. Entering the lady's room, he was mesmerized by the utter serenity of this woman who, bedridden for several years, was now facing the end with a smiling countenance. The nurse scribbled the whispered instructions of the stricken woman for the disposal of her property. When all three witnesses had signed the paper, the lady smiled, thanked them and said, "And now I am ready to leave this pain-wracked body to meet my Maker, my husband, my father, my mother, and all my friends who have gone before me. Won't that be wonderful!"

Tears started down Benham's pale, wrinkled cheeks. "Look at me," he said in a hoarse whisper. "I've lain awake many nights since I learned my days were numbered, staring at the ceiling with nothing to look forward to except that my life would end in a handful of ashes. That's the difference between me, an atheist, and the lady I've described. She, believing, faces her final days with a smile. Here am I, a nonbeliever, with every moment a nightmare, facing nothing but a cold tomb." He hesitated a few moments, then added, "I would shove my hands into a bed of red-hot coals if by so doing I could secure a belief in a Supreme Being and an afterlife!"

Death—A Dreadful Enemy
Death is a terrible enemy. It plays no favorites, has a key to every home, cares not for our plans, often beckoning the young before the old and the strong before the weak. Every newspaper carries his advertisement; every tombstone is his pulpit.

Who can deny Ben Franklin's observation, "In this world nothing can be said to be certain, except death and taxes." Whether we meet death on a highway or spend our final years in a senior citizens' playground, Sir Walter Scott put it,
> And come he slow, or come he fast,
> It is but Death who comes at last.
> —Marmion, II 30

## HOPE IN THE FACE OF DEATH

Death was not a part of God's original creation. All that God created was good. Adam was warned, "In the day that you eat of [the forbidden fruit] you shall die" (Gen. 2:17, RSV). When Adam disobeyed, he was expelled from the garden and told he would return to dust (3:19, 23). Death, a consequence of sin, has been passed on to all men (Rom. 5:12). Every person since Adam has died or will, except for Enoch and Elijah, who were translated. "The last enemy that shall be destroyed is death" (1 Cor. 15:26).

When our time is up, we cannot postpone it. It is said that Andrew Carnegie once offered a million dollars to any doctor who could prolong his life by ten years, but no one could so guarantee. In that famed *New England Primer* used to teach school children the alphabet, the maxim under A read: "In Adam's fall we sinned all." Under X: "*X*erxes the great died, and so must you and I."

An Easterner, searching the wide open spaces of the West for a healthy place to live, approached an old man in a small Arizona town. He asked, "What's the death rate around here?" Came the answer, "Same as back east—one to a person."

I shall never forget the first funeral I conducted. A student at Moody Bible Institute, I was sent out to conduct the service of a 24-year-old girl. Her four small children couldn't grasp the significance of what was happening. Though her husband grieved bravely, it was her mother who sorrowed the most. As the funeral director began to close the casket, her mother screamed over and over these piercing words I shall never forget: "Never—see her—again! NEVER——SEE HER—AGAIN!"

### Avoidance of Death
It has been reported that King James I of England allowed no one to enter his gate with mourning clothes, and that journal-

ist William Randolph Hearst forbad the mention of death in his presence. Some react to a doctor's verdict of terminal illness with silence, refusing to accept it or talk about it. Young people sometimes put off contemplation of death saying, "I'll cross that bridge when I come to it. What will happen will happen. Nothing I can do will change it. Why worry?"

The *Christian Science Monitor* refuses to print the word *death* in its columns. Our attempts to evade thoughts of death are shown in our euphemisms. Death becomes *leave-taking*. A corpse is a *loved one*. People do not die; they *expire*. Undertakers are termed *funeral directors*. Coffins are called *caskets*. The deceased are made to look as alive as possible, laid out in a slumber room with an organ playing soft music. Hearses are called *coaches* or *professional cars*.

Perhaps the thought of facing God in judgment makes some seek diversion in order to drown out the thought of death. It has been said that Americans have built a billion dollar industry to help them forget about death—the entertainment business. German theologian Helmut Thielicke once said that because New Year's reminds us that life is slipping away, people must make noise "to drown out the macabre sound of grass growing over their graves."

Some even try to evade death at the very moment of its arrival. Psychiatrists have done serious study in the relationship between LSD and dying, because this drug has seemed to offer some sort of a cure to the ultimate fear. In his novel *Island,* Aldous Huxley describes the death of a character on psychedelic drugs. Not surprisingly, the night Huxley himself was dying, his wife administered LSD to him.

By dying and rising from the grave, Christ destroyed the power of death (2 Tim. 1:10). He did not underestimate its dreadfulness, but confronted it directly, determined to crush its cruel grip. When He became obedient unto death, wicked hands could do no more. Christ snatched from the devil the keys of death. The grave could not confine His body. An angel rolled back the stone and sat on it to show that death had been defied (Matt. 28:2). To further display His power over death, and as a token of His dominion over the tomb in the coming resurrection day, Christ brought several saints back to life. These saints went into Jerusalem and appeared to many in what must have been a grand reunion (Matt. 27:52-53).

Because of Christ's victory we exclaim with Paul, "O death, where is thy sting? O grave, where is thy victory?" (1 Cor. 15:55). To counteract the strategy of the devil whose game-plan from the beginning has been leading people into sin, and thus into death, Christ through death has destroyed "him that had the power of death, that is, the devil" and delivered "them who through fear of death were all their lifetime subject to bondage" (Heb. 2:14-15).

When Dr. Donald Barnhouse was driving to his wife's funeral service with his four children in the car, a huge truck pulled past them, throwing its shadow across the car. He asked the children, "Would you rather be run over by a truck or by the shadow of a truck?" The eleven-year-old replied, "The shadow, of course." Dr. Barnhouse said, "That's what happened to your mother. Only the shadow of death has passed over her, because death itself ran over Jesus. But He rose, and lives, and so does she in heaven."

## What Is Death to the Believer?

For the believer, death is a transition, not a termination. Three of the nouns used for death in the New Testament suggest that death is a commencement not a conclusion, a comma instead of a period.

*Sleep.* Jesus told the disciples that He was returning to Bethany to wake Lazarus out of sleep (John 11:11). Dead saints are described as those "which sleep in Jesus" (1 Cor. 11:30;

15:20, 51; 1 Thes. 4:13-14). Jesus and Paul were not teaching the doctrine of soul sleep, but merely noting the similarity between sleep and death. Homer wrote, "Sleep is the twin of death."

Sleep is but for a while. We expect to wake soon, refreshed for the tasks of the new day. Death is going to sleep down here in the shadows, and awakening over there immediately in the glorious light of eternal dawn.

A farmer took his little son on a visit to a distant village. Along the way they came to a swift stream, spanned by a rickety old bridge, which frightened the little lad, even though it was daylight. Returning at dusk, the boy recalled the stream and old bridge, and became panicky. How would they cross that turbulent stream in the dark? Noting his anxiety, the father lifted the boy and carried him in his arms. Before they reached the bridge, he was fast asleep against his father's shoulder. As the next morning's sun streamed in his bedroom window, the boy awoke to discover he was safe at home. At death the believer falls asleep in the Saviour's arms to awaken in His bright land of no night and no fear.

*Exodus.* A second New Testament noun used of death is *exodus,* virtually the same in both Greek and English. Speaking of his own death, Peter reminded his readers of truths he wanted them to recall after his decease, literally, exodus (2 Peter 1:15).

This word would make Peter's readers think of the exodus of the Israelites, marking their passage through the Red Sea and deliverance from the bondage of Egypt. Along life's path Christians are hounded by all sorts of relentless enemies right to the last gasp. Then suddenly a Christian passes through the waters of death, leaving his enemies behind forever.

*Departure.* The third New Testament word for death is *departure.* Paul's last recorded words included "the time of my departure is at hand" (2 Tim. 4:6). This word is used in various ways. It may refer to the *unloosing* of a prisoner at the moment of release. Death brings freedom from chains. It is also used for the solution or *unravelling* of a problem or *opening* of a lock. Death will illuminate what we have not understood before, and help us penetrate some mysteries. It is sometimes used for the *breaking up* of a banquet, the *breaking* of camp by a company of soldiers, and for the *raising* of an anchor, which permits the departure of a ship.

When giant ships used to ply the oceans, great excitement prevailed a few minutes before leaving: pandemonium of farewells, bustle of loading, beating of gongs to warn visitors to leave. Then the gangplank was raised, the anchor weighed, and the ship glided slowly out to sea as final greetings were waved. How often Paul had experienced anchors aweigh on his voyage from port to port around the Mediterranean.

Embarkation from one harbor assumes arrival at another. Our departure from earth at death presupposes entrance to our heavenly destination. Some believe the "abundant entrance" of 2 Peter 1:11 is language borrowed from the arrival of passengers at port on a pleasant afternoon, with flags flying and crowds lined up to greet relatives and friends. Hymns speak of "crossing the swelling tide" and of landing "safe on that beautiful shore."

Different Reactions at Death
When infidel Tom Payne was dying, he was heard to utter, "O Lord, help! O our Lord Jesus Christ, help!" His surprised doctor asked, "What's this I hear? Tom Payne, a man who spent his life ridiculing the Christian faith and scoffing at the Lord Jesus Christ. As your physician, I ask you as a dying man, do you now repent of your infidel views and turn to this Christ for salvation?" Payne replied, "No, I cannot believe on that man." He died, still an unbeliever.

## THE SUSTAINING POWER OF HOPE

The famous anthropologist, Margaret Mead, born in 1901, died of cancer in 1978. Her husband, Gregory, three years younger, also died of cancer in 1980. A *New York Times* book review (Aug. 18, 1984) states that though Mead had always insisted that life should include an acknowledgment of death, she refused against undeniable evidence to admit that she was dying, but engaged a "healer" to treat her. Gregory died a planned death, "surrounded by Zen students meditating day and night." The reviewer observed that when the end came, neither of these renowned scientists found science or rationality much help in facing the unknown.

But when the Scottish preacher John Knox was dying, he took his wife's hand and asked, "Read to me that Scripture on which I first cast my anchor." In her last illness hymn writer Fanny Crosby remarked, "How can anyone call it a dark valley? It is all light and love." The dying words of Adoniram Judson, first missionary to Burma, were, "I go with the gladness of a boy bounding away from school. I feel so strong in Christ."

On her deathbed, Susanna Wesley uttered this last request before losing her speech, "Children, as soon as I am released, sing a psalm of praise to God." When her son, John Wesley, was about to die in his 88th year in extreme weakness, he astonished his friends by breaking out singing a stanza of a hymn which began, "I'll praise my Maker while I've breath."

When D.L. Moody was rushed home to Massachusetts after a sudden illness during a western crusade, he said to his son, "Earth recedes, heaven opens before me. If this is death, it is sweet. There is no valley here. God is calling me, and I must go. This is my coronation day. It is glorious."

### When Loved Ones Die
What a misconception that Christians should not weep when believing loved ones die. Perhaps 1 Thessalonians 4:13 contrib-

utes to this false notion. It reads: "But I would not have you to be ignorant, brethren, concerning them which are asleep, that ye sorrow not, even as others which have no hope." But the comma, not in the original, has been misplaced by the translator and should be moved back so as to read, "that ye sorrow, not even as others which have no hope." The *New International Version* tells us not to "grieve like the rest of men, who have no hope."

Sorrow is natural when we lose a loved one. The devout men who carried Stephen to his burial "made great lamentation over him" (Acts 8:2). When Dorcas died, the widows stood around crying (9:39). At the tomb of Lazarus, Jesus wept (John 11:35). Today when death reaches its icy fingers into a home and makes us long for the touch of a vanished hand, and the sound of a voice that is still, sorrow is only natural. However, for the believer, natural sorrow is accompanied by supernatural hope.

Since the Lord created us with the desire for self-preservation, naturally we have some apprehension when we stop to contemplate our death. A Christian, in the best of health, confessed, "I don't think I possess dying grace." His friend answered, "You don't need it when you're living. When it's time to go, you'll be given it."

Noted lexicographer Dr. Samuel Johnson was an earnest Christian, yet he had a deep horror of death. According to his biographer, James Boswell, Johnson's fear of death stemmed from his fear of judgment. When reminded of the merits of his Redeemer, Johnson replied, "I do not forget the merits of my Redeemer; but my Redeemer said that He will set some on His right hand and some on His left." However, when Johnson came to die, he was able to face the enemy with calm because his strong fear was overcome by a deeper hope. So it should be for all who anchor their hope in Christ's forgiveness as promised in His Word.

# THE SUSTAINING POWER OF HOPE

## Some Questions to Ask Ourselves

A girl in her early twenties, dying after a car accident, gasped these final words to her mother, "Mother, you taught me everything I needed to know to get by in college. You taught me how to light my cigarette, how to hold my cocktail glass, and how to use the pill. But Mother, you never taught me how to die. You'd better teach me quickly, Mother, because I'm dying!"

First, we should ask ourselves, *Am I right in my relationship with God? Have I received His Son as my Saviour?* We should not wait until our deathbed to settle this question. We have no guarantee of life tomorrow, or of having a lingering death.

Second, we should ask ourselves, *Am I right in my relationship with my family, my friends, and my Christian co-workers: Does some relationship need to be reconciled?*

Finally, we should ask ourselves, *Am I living with eternity's values in view, or is my main ambition slanted toward money, fame, hobby, pleasure, or some other empty idol?*

We *can* face death victoriously. Sami Dagher, pastor of Karantina Alliance Church in war-torn Beirut, Lebanon, wrote, "When I kiss my wife good-bye in the morning, I know that we may not see each other again. If there is no shooting, if there are no bombs, then we are still afraid of car bombs. Recently, just before I went on a trip, two armed men broke into our home and threatened our lives. I thought about canceling the trip, but my wife said to me, 'Remember, if anything happens to us in your absence, we will be with the Lord.'"

# NINE
# THE BLESSED HOPE

THE FIRST NIGHT an inflatable sphere was launched from Wallops Island, Virginia, residents of the area had no advance notice. Conjectures ran wild when the bright light flashed in the sky.

"It's the Russians!"

"Men from Mars!"

"An exploding star!"

As the spectacle loomed brighter, one woman gasped, "Maybe it's the coming of the Lord!"

"Oh my!" exclaimed her neighbor, a very fussy housekeeper. "I do hope He doesn't come to my home first!"

Someday Jesus will rend the skies to rescue this old world out of its present mess. When He returns in majesty, all nations will kneel before Him as He institutes His rule on earth, bringing order out of chaos, and peace out of strife. Anticipation of great times ahead is anchored in the hope of His coming, when He will also raise the dead believers, transform the living saints, giving all believers perfect bodies. (See 1 Cor. 15:40, 42-44, 51-52; Phil. 3:21.)

### Fact of His Second Coming

The Bible teaches that Jesus Christ is coming to earth again. How logical for Him to be vindicated on this very planet where at His first coming He was shamefully rejected. He Himself said He would return: "If I go and prepare a place for you, I will come again, and receive you unto Myself; that where I am, there ye may be also" (John 14:3).

At our Lord's ascension from the Mount of Olives, two angels said to the disciples, "Ye men of Galilee, why stand ye gazing up into heaven? This same Jesus, which is taken up from you into heaven, shall so come in like manner as ye have seen Him go into heaven" (Acts 1:11). Our Lord went up visibly, bodily, and personally. He will return to us in the same manner.

Paul wrote with unmistakable clarity, "The Lord Himself shall descend from heaven with a shout, with the voice of the archangel, and with the trump of God; and the dead in Christ shall rise first; then we which are alive and remain shall be caught up together with them in the clouds, to meet the Lord in the air; and so shall we ever be with the Lord" (1 Thes. 4:16-17).

The last book in the Bible, as its title indicates, deals with the appearing or revelation of Jesus Christ. In the opening chapter John wrote, "Behold, He cometh with clouds; and every eye shall see Him, and they also which pierced Him; and all kindreds of the earth shall wail because of Him" (Rev. 1:7). In the last chapter is John's prayer for the Lord's return, "Even so, come, Lord Jesus" (Rev. 22:20).

If the approximately 300 references to the Second Coming in the New Testament were spaced equidistantly through twenty-seven books, it is estimated that every twenty-five verses we would hear Jesus say, "I am coming again."

Many copies of the "Battle Hymn of the Republic" omit the final stanza which refers to the Second Coming:

> He is coming like the glory
> Of the morning on the wave;
> He is wisdom to the mighty,
> He is succor to the brave;
> So the world shall be His footstool,
> And the soul of time His slave;
> Our God is marching on.

### Personal, Visible, Bodily Return

Many attempt to explain the Second Coming as something other than the personal, visible, and bodily return of Christ to earth. For instance, some people spiritualize it as the progressive development of Christian principles through the world till society is permeated with the Gospel. They suggest it means that divine love will win out and victory over evil will be complete. However, the Bible speaks of the Second Coming as taking place in the twinkling of an eye, and as suddenly as the flashing of lightning from east to west. Whoever heard of gradual lightning?

Some claim that Pentecost was the Second Coming. But the New Testament promises of His return were penned after Pentecost. Besides, it was the Holy Spirit that came on the Day of Pentecost, not the Lord Jesus.

Others affirm that death is the Second Coming, at which time Christ comes for the believer. In a limited sense this is true, but at death Christ does not come visibly nor bodily. Also, death is a hated enemy, whereas Christ's return is a comforting concept. Substituting *death* in verses which speak of Christ's return will destroy the sense of the verse. For example, we are not taught to watch for death, but rather for His coming.

When Japanese forces invaded the Philippines in 1942, General Douglas MacArthur was forced to withdraw. On leaving, he made a famous promise, "I shall return." For the next few years

Filipinos and Americans tasted the bitterness of war. But they had the promise of a trusted leader which gave them hope. In 1945 troops under MacArthur's command did capture those lost Pacific islands and freed the surviving Americans and Filipinos.

On His first visit to this world Jesus Christ was crucified. But He has promised to return to this very scene of His rejection, where then every knee will bow before Him and every tongue confess that He is Lord.

### Time of the Second Coming

No one knows when Jesus Christ is coming back. The person who sets a date contradicts Jesus who said, "But of that day and hour knoweth no man, no, not the angels of heaven, but My Father only" (Matt. 24:36). In almost every generation, date-setters have brought this doctrine into disrepute. A century and a half ago a group in New York sold their possessions, gowned themselves in white, and climbed to tops of hills to await Christ's return. But He never came. They claimed a miscalculation and reset the date for a year later. Again, He did not come.

Though our world seems to stagger from one crisis to another, almost every generation has wondered if it would survive. In 1848 Lord Shaftesbury said, "Nothing can save the [British] Empire from shipwreck." In 1849 Disraeli commented, "In industry, commerce, and agriculture there is no hope." In 1852 the dying Duke of Wellington said, "I thank God I shall be spared from seeing the consummation of ruin that is gathering about us."

*Harper's Weekly* in October 1857 reported, "It is a gloomy moment of history. Not for many years—not for a lifetime of most men who read this—has there been so much grave and deep apprehension; never has the future seemed so incalculable.... Of our troubles no one can see the end."

Through the years prophetic teachers have pointed out signs which seemed to portend the end of the age: wars and rumors of wars (Matt. 24:6), famines (24:7), earthquakes (24:7), knowledge explosion (Dan. 12:4), increased travel and speed (12:4), apostasy (2 Thes. 2:3), and widespread immorality (2 Tim. 3:1-4). Though these may well signal the end time, perhaps the following three signs indicate His return could be soon.

*Israel's Restoration.* Many Bible students understand Scripture to teach a future for Israel which requires the Jews to be back in their homeland. A red-letter day in Jewish history occurred on December 11, 1917, when Palestine's door was opened to the Jews by British General Edmund Allenby's triumphal entry into Jerusalem. In the 1920s I heard my pastors declare repeatedly what seemed an impossibility, namely that the Jews would return to Palestine as a national homeland. The dream became a reality on May 14, 1948 when the state of Israel was established. On May 11, 1949 Israel became a member of the United Nations. Today over 2 million people reside in Israel.

After nineteen centuries without a national state, persecuted, scattered into every nation around the globe, and 6 million murdered in the Holocaust, that the Jew should maintain his identity and now possess his own national state is indeed a miracle. Though admitting that this present set-up could linger for decades, the situation also sets the stage for the possible nearness of Christ's return.

*Global Adhesiveness.* One hundred and fifty years ago few people knew what the President of the United States looked like. The first motion picture of a president was filmed in 1897 as President Grover Cleveland accompanied President-elect William McKinley to his inauguration. McKinley appeared only three times before newsreel cameras. Teddy Roosevelt became well-known through the newsreel. While Franklin Roosevelt reached the nation through his fireside chats, Harry Truman was the first to make a telecast from the White House. Dwight Eisenhower was the first to permit an entire press conference to be recorded by TV cameras. John Kennedy's funeral dominated TV programming for three full days, and was relayed to many nations around the world through the Telstar satellite.

Science has shrunk our world so that planes fly from one continent to another in a few short hours. What happens in Hong Kong or Iran or Argentina is flashed on our TV newscasts a few hours later, which makes for one small world. This "one world" aspect makes it easy for the rise of world domination by one nation, and the emergence of a dictator to become the Antichrist. If the Antichrist could be seen at one time through modern mass communications, so could the Second Coming of Christ. When Neil Armstrong stepped on to the moon, over 100 million people from all parts of the world watched. Though God's omnipotence could make Christ visible to all the world at one time apart from the use of technology, man's ability to telecast pictures to all the world simultaneously makes us realize that the Second Coming could be viewed by all nations at one time.

This global adhesiveness helps the worldwide missionary movement. The first modern missionary society was founded by William Carey in 1792. Jesus said that the Gospel "shall be preached in all the world for a witness unto all nations; and then shall the end come" (Matt. 24:14). Our advancing communications expertise should speed up the task of world evangelization, and thus make Christ's coming imminent.

*Indifference.* Another end-time characteristic will be indifference to Gospel truth. "As the days of Noah were, so shall also the coming of the Son of man be. For as in the days that were before the flood they were eating and drinking, marrying and giving in marriage, until the day that Noah entered into the ark, and knew not until the flood came, and took them all away; so shall also the coming of the Son of man be" (Matt. 24:37-

39). Though Noah's generation spawned much violence and immorality, perhaps those irregularities stemmed from indifference to God's truth.

Jesus was saying that people would go through the routines of life, eating meals, getting married, but giving little or no thought to eternal matters. They philosophized, "The sun rose yesterday. It rose today. Of course, it will rise tomorrow." Today, vast numbers are indifferent to God's name, church, Son, Word, and work. The coming of Christ will catch many unaware. The indifference of our day fits the spirit of neglect which will prevail at the time of Christ's return.

The saintly Murray McCheyne of Scotland was hosting a ministers' meeting in his home. In a lull in the conversation he asked the ministers individually, "Do you think Jesus will come tonight?" All said, "No, I think not." After going the rounds and receiving the same answer, McCheyne solemnly repeated, "Therefore be ye also ready; for in such an hour as ye think not the Son of man cometh" (Matt. 24:44).

### Effects of This Hope

For the unbeliever, the teaching on the Second Coming brings no hope, only terror. Paul wrote, "The Lord Jesus shall be revealed from heaven with His mighty angels, in flaming fire taking vengeance on them that know not God, and that obey not the Gospel of our Lord Jesus Christ; who shall be punished with everlasting destruction from the presence of the Lord, and from the glory of His power (2 Thes. 1:7-9). Also, says Paul, "He shall come to be glorified in His saints" (v. 10).

*Encouragement to troubled hearts.* When Jesus told His disciples, "Let not your heart be troubled," He linked it with, "I will come again, and receive you unto Myself" (John 14:1, 3). The Second Coming is the point at which much of the believer's guaranteed hope will come into full blossom, including resurrection of the body and reunion with loved ones.

The coming of the Prince of Peace will usher in an era of tranquility to this troubled, tortured world. Peace shall cover the earth as the waters cover the sea. The lion and the lamb will lie down together (Isa. 11:6; 65:25). Swords will be beaten into plowshares and spears into pruninghooks (Isa. 2:4). Nations shall not lift up sword against nation. Violence and injustice will be eliminated, and universal brotherhood will prevail.

*Incentive to faithful service.* Jesus said, "Behold, I come as a thief. Blessed is he that watcheth" (Rev. 16:15). We do not watch for the Lord by gazing skyward, or by forever studying prophecy or making hair-splitting exegesis on eschatological texts, or by attacking every brother who doesn't agree with our chart of coming events. The real meaning of *watch* is to be up and at it, doing our Christian task. If your boss, before leaving on a business trip, assigned you a job to complete in his absence, genuine watching for your boss' return would not mean standing at the window, looking for his car to drive up the street, but performing the assigned task.

Jesus said, "Who then is a faithful and wise servant? . . . Blessed is that servant, whom his lord when he cometh shall find so doing. Verily I say unto you, that he shall make him ruler over all his goods." Then He told of the punishment awaiting the negligent servant (Matt. 24:45-51). The hope of the Second Coming provides a powerful incentive to faithful service.

*Motivation to holy living.* A student in Bible college worked part-time for a company with many expensive tools. On several occasions, the student took tools to keep for himself. One day his doctrine teacher assigned the student to write a paper on the Second Coming. As he worked on it, the student became deeply convicted of his stealing, especially by the verse, "When He shall appear, we shall be like Him; for we shall see Him as He is. And every man that hath this hope in him purifieth himself, even as He is pure" (1 John 3:2-3). Summoning courage, he went to his boss with the stolen tools and confessed his theft, expecting to be fired, perhaps even arrested. Instead, the boss asked the student to stay on, remarking, "You're the type of employee I want."

Because of our abiding hope, believers ought to be better citizens down here, filled with concern and compassion for the less fortunate. Not only should this hope produce love for the temporal welfare of our fellowmen, but should also produce a strong desire to see them enjoy the same precious hope through Christ's redeeming grace.

This purifying hope has to reach into the very core of our lifestyles and moral standards. A group of American artists lived in a little colony in Rome, finishing their studies. An older, wealthy man was sort of a patron to all of the artists. He himself had failed in the art world, so went into business and made a fortune, which he spent to help young Americans finish their training to be what he had hoped to be.

He noticed a certain young fellow who kept himself aloof from the debauches in which all the others indulged from time to time. Every excuse for a celebration, like Memorial Day or July 4, occasioned a hilarious drinking and licentious party. But this one young artist did not enter into these wild affairs. Just the same he was a well-liked fellow, respected by the others because of his helpful attitude.

After watching this young man for two years, the older man took him on a walk up one of the seven hills of Rome just at sunset, as a crimson mass of clouds glowed in the western sky. After ten minutes of silence, hushed by the beauty of the sunset, the old man said, "I've been watching you for two years now, and I cannot help noticing that you hold yourself aloof from those parties the others have so often. I cannot help but feel there's something in your life that helps you do that. Would you tell me what it is?"

## THE SUSTAINING POWER OF HOPE

The young artist looked up into the old man's face, then into the glowing sunset. "Over westward beyond that sunset lies America, and in a little New England village there is a home, and in that home lives the girl I love. I'm keeping myself clean for her."

Surrounded by an evil culture and an adulterous generation, we should live for our Saviour and for the day when He comes to claim us for His own.

# ❧ TEN ❧
# THE FOUNTAIN OF YOUTH

*Psychology Today* posed this question in its December 1983 issue: "If someone offered you a pill that would make it possible for you to live 500 years, would you take it?"

Thirteen hundred men and women, ranging in age from 13 to 95, responded with a wide array of answers. Many men said they would like to live 500 years to achieve and learn more. Some wanted more time to make money. Others wondered if the government could pay Social Security for 435 years, or would they have to work until they reached the age of 465. Women also wanted to live longer in order to accomplish more, or to see if the future would turn out as the fiction writers had pictured. On the other hand, many objected to longevity, fearing centuries of suffering, senility, or fading beauty.

If mankind could stay forever young while advancing in years, he would probably want to live forever. Man has ever searched for the fountain of youth. In the last two decades over 800 U.S. research teams have studied the possibility of increasing man's lifespan and vigor in old age. The U.S. Department of Health has spent over $7 million on a new institute of gerontology which hopes to tamper directly with the timing mechanism which brings on the onset of old age.

The search for the fountain of youth is not new. Every school child has heard of Ponce de Leon, a Spanish explorer and companion of Columbus. According to legend, Ponce de Leon was sent to conquer the island of Puerto Rico, where amassing a huge fortune, he learned of land to the north with waters which supposedly could confer perennial youth on those who bathed or drank there. Setting out with three ships he discovered a country in 1513, which he called Florida (flowers). But he failed to find the fountain of perpetual youth.

Though medical science has extended our life expectancy from 70.2 years in 1965 to 74.5 years in 1983, and could raise it to 80 years by 2000, it is not opening up the fountain of youth. Rather, medical advances are adding millions of old people to the population. One fishing enthusiast exclaimed, "The waters of the fountain of youth are all around me." Doubtless, trout streams are therapeutic, but fishermen die. The mortality rate is still and always will be 100 percent.

For many, growing old is the worst of tragedies. Panic sets in at mid-life with the realization that because vim, vigor, and vitality aren't as plentiful, they cannot keep up the pace of a few years previous. This is why many are obsessed with youth. Ads and commercials lead us to believe that eating, drinking, driving, shopping, and swimming are all done only by pretty girls and handsome men under 30. A most cherished compliment is to tell a lady she does not look her age. The cult of youth has muscled its way into the lives of middle-aged executives who become addicts of gymnasiums, cosmetic companies, and hair salons. Men can have their hair waved and sprayed, their eyebrows tinted, and their wrinkles removed by a youth facial. Women go to fine restaurants to order Melba toast, chicken broth, and grapefruit, not just to prevent middle-age spread, but out of fear of growing old. Helen Hayes in her book, *A Gift of Joy,* says the effort to hold back the clock is one of the most pathetic efforts in which people engage.

Then what's ahead for us? Growing older and older, feebler and weaker, then death and the grave—and that's it? Is there no fountain of youth—no hope? The Bible speaks of life after death where our joy shall overflow, love abound, strength renew, and the old shall be young forever. The resurrection story in the Book of Mark suggests a hint in our quest for the fountain of youth. When the women reached the empty tomb that first Easter morning, they saw "a young man sitting on the right side" (Mark 16:5). He was one of two angels at the tomb (Luke 24:4; John 20:12). But it was his youthfulness that was noted. He was a visitor from the realm of the heavenlies and eternities, and he was *young.*

### Young in Appearance

The women at the tomb were impressed by the angel's youthful appearance. The word here for "young man" is used of one in the prime of life. The same noun is applied to the rich young ruler (Matt. 19:22); to the young fellow (probably Mark) who fled at Jesus' arrest (Mark 14:51); to the young man Jesus raised from his coffin during a burial procession (Luke 7:14); to the young men who carried out Ananias and later Sapphira (Acts 5:6, 10); to the young man (Saul) who guarded the clothes of Stephen's killers (7:58); to Paul's nephew (23:17-18, 22); and to the class of youth intermediate between children and father (1 John 2:13-14).

So many symbols of Easter speak of life at its most beautiful period. The caterpillar, which leaves its pupa to soar upward as a butterfly, suggests the lovely new life into which His followers will be raised. Likewise, from the bulb which decays in the ground a new, radiant lily is released.

The peacock also symbolizes the resurrection because of the

annual renewal of its brilliant plumage. New grass, new clothes, new life hatched from eggs, all signify the emergence of new and youthful-looking life.

At what age will we appear to be in our glorified bodies? As we looked at 10, 30, 50, or 70? Doesn't this angelic visitor's youthful appearance give us a strong hint? Will we not appear as we looked in the prime of life?

Had we been on the Mount of Transfiguration with Peter, James, and John, we would likely have seen Moses and Elijah as they appeared at the height of their youthful manhood. The Lord Jesus received His glorified body in the prime of life. In our resurrected bodies we will probably look as we did at the zenith of our earthly life, since our bodies will be fashioned like unto His glorious and youthful body.

**Young in Mind**

Youth is the golden age of memory. Attempts to memorize poetry or Bible verses after mid-life usually prove more difficult. How often older people exclaim, "I just can't remember as I used to."

Young people also learn more quickly than senior citizens. A new missionary in a foreign culture wrote home that his children were mastering the language much more speedily than their parents, because their youthful minds picked it up so easily.

The young man at Jesus' tomb knew a great deal. He knew that the disciples were seeking Jesus and that they were afraid. He predicted they would see Jesus in Galilee. He reminded them that Jesus had prophesied His crucifixion and resurrection. He was cognizant of Peter's despair, as indicated by his request to the women to specifically tell Peter of Jesus' rising from the dead (Mark 16:7).

The superiority of angelic knowledge over man's is implied in

# THE FOUNTAIN OF YOUTH

Jesus' statement that the date of His Second Coming was not known even by angels (Mark 13:32). But someday we shall know more than the angels. How much knowledge there will be to learn in heaven! Down here college students can barely scrape the surface of their major fields. Scholars have to specialize until "they know more and more about less and less until they know everything about nothing." A mathematics professor named his retirement cottage "Aftermath," hoping to find time to pursue science, psychology, literature, and a host of subjects in which he was interested. Eternity will provide lots of time to search out knowledge now beyond our grasp. To help us learn, God's people will possess, along with their glorified bodies, alert and youthful minds.

Not only does youth learn more easily, but it has a zest for learning. Some maintain this alert outlook through old age. An old body may house a young mind. When Alexander Graham Bell was 75, a friend commented, "The most remarkable thing about Dr. Bell is that he is younger in mind than most men half his age. Mentally he seems to have discovered a fountain of youth which keeps him perennially alert and vigorous." Bell followed three rules of study: observe, remember, and compare—principles which belong to a youthful outlook on life.

Sick with the grippe in his eighties, former Chancellor of West Germany Konrad Adenauer was told by his doctor, "I cannot make you young again." Eager to get back in harness, Adenauer replied, "I'm not asking that. I don't wish to become young again. All I want is to go on getting older!" Carl Sandburg commented, "It's not a bad practice for a man of many years to die with a boy's heart."

Youth views life adventurously and enthusiastically, and does not bore quickly. To the child a bowl of cereal may portray a city surrounded by a moat, or rearranged by his spoon, a lake surrounded by a wall. Children amuse themselves in simple ways. The person who loses zest and possesses fewer interests reflects aging. Ralph Waldo Emerson wrote, "We do not count a man's years until he has nothing else to count." On the other hand, one Christian gentleman exclaimed with sparkling eyes, "It's fun to be 75 and the Lord's." Perhaps he was subconsciously anticipating the youthful outlook with which the fountain of youth would endue him in the world to come.

The possibility of staying youthful on the inside while aging on the outside is illustrated in the creative accomplishments of older men. John Milton wrote *Paradise Regained* at 63. Noah Webster wrote his monumental dictionary at 70. Socrates gave his wise philosophies at 70. Ignace Paderewski still gave concerts before large audiences at 79. William Gladstone still presented a powerful figure in political circles at 80. Benjamin Franklin helped to frame the U.S. constitution at 81. Johann von Goethe completed *Faust* at 82. Thomas Edison worked busily in his lab at 83. Alfred Tennyson published his memorable poem, *Crossing the Bar,* at 83. Guiseppe Verdi was 85 when he composed *Te Deum.* Michelangelo was in his late 80s when he painted some of his masterpieces. Arturo Toscanini conducted an orchestra at 87. Grandma Moses did many of her paintings after 90.

At a denomination's annual conference, special recognition was given an elderly but exuberant man. At 65 he had retired from the University of California where he was a specialist in fruit trees. With fresh ideas on pruning, he opened an orchard of his own in the Pacific Northwest. After clearing $100,000 in the next dozen years, he returned to southern California and was licensed as a local preacher to start new churches.

For twelve years he averaged one new church a year. Establishing each new church involved selecting the site, negotiating the loan, raising the money, and visiting the prospective members. At 89 he was asked, "How many house visits do you average a year?" He offhandedly replied, "Anywhere from 3,500 to 5,000." Then he added, "It's a great way to prove you're alive.

## THE FOUNTAIN OF YOUTH

But I'm having a bit of trouble now. Sometimes I get lightheaded on my rounds and fall over in a faint. But it's not so bad. The jar brings me to and clears my head. I just pick myself up, brush off the dust, and go on!"

**Young in Strength**
Vigor declines with the passing of years. Some doggerel puts it:

> How do I know my youth is all spent?
> Well, my get up and go has got up and went.
> But in spite of it all, I am able to grin
> When I think of the places my get up has been.
> Old age is golden, so I've heard it said
> But sometimes I wonder as I get into bed.
>
> With my ears in a drawer, my teeth in a cup,
> My eyes on the table, until I wake up.
> Ere sleep dims my eyes, I say to myself,
> *Is there anything else I should put on the shelf?*
> And I'm happy to say as I close my door
> My friends are the same, or perhaps even more.
>
> When I was young my slippers were red.
> I could kick up my heels right over my head.
> When I grew older, my slippers were blue,
> But still I could dance the whole night through.
> Now that I'm old, my slippers are black,
> I walk to the store and puff my way back.
> The reason I know my youth is all spent,
> My get up and go has got up and went.
>
> But I really don't mind, and I think with a grin
> Of all the places my get up has been.

# THE SUSTAINING POWER OF HOPE

> Since I have retired from life's competition,
> I busy myself with complete repetition,
> I get up each morning, dust off my wits,
> Pick up my paper and read the obits.
> If my name is still missing, I know I'm not dead.
> So I eat a good breakfast and go back to bed.
> —Author unknown

Youth is the age of energy and athletics. The Olympic record holders are young. A star hockey player retired from the game because he was getting a little clumsy, more easily tired, and not responding as quickly as in earlier years. John wrote, "I have written unto you, young men, because ye are strong" (1 John 2:14). Says Proverbs, "The glory of young men is their strength" (Prov. 20:29).

The young man by the empty tomb that first Easter morning exercised superhuman strength in rolling back the heavy stone from the door. The guards were so afraid that they shook and became like dead men, doubtless awed in part by the power of the angel which moved a stone that normally took several muscular men to budge.

Though two angels were mentioned, probably no more than one was needed to destroy Sodom and Gomorrah (Gen. 19:1). One angel slew 185,000 Assyrians (Isa. 37:36). One angel released Peter from prison, knocking off his chains and opening the iron gate (Acts 12:7, 10). One angel will be powerful enough to lay hold of Satan and cast him into the bottomless pit (Rev. 20:1-2). Though not *almighty,* angels are *mighty* (2 Thes. 1:7).

Angels may exceed the Christian in strength now, but someday redeemed and glorified man will surpass angels in power. Sown in weakness, the Christian corpse will be "raised in power" (1 Cor. 15:43). Believers will be fashioned like unto Christ's resurrected body (Phil. 3:21). On the first Easter,

## THE FOUNTAIN OF YOUTH

Christ covered much distance in speedy fashion, appearing to Mary, to the women along the way, somewhere to Peter, to the Emmaus disciples as He walked several miles with them, then many miles back to the Upper Room in Jerusalem, even passing through closed doors. Like His risen body, our glorified bodies will be able to move with velocity, and ascend without the help of a space suit or launching pad.

All deformities and infirmities of our present bodies will be erased. The aches of age, the pains of arthritis, the panting of cardiacs, the wheezing of emphysema victims, the shuffling of the semi-paralyzed will never bother the resurrected bodies of believers. No feeble nor invalid will languish in old peoples' homes, nursing homes, welfare homes, state hospitals, or any kind of hospitals. Varied and strange maladies strike the body here. There, the fountain of youth will maintain permanent health and vitality.

A college football coach was asked to tell one of his players of the death of the boy's father. In the locker room the coach found the boy and broke the news to him. He told the boy to take a week off. As it was Tuesday, the coach didn't expect to see him again till the following week.

But on Friday, three days later, the coach found the player in the locker room, suiting up for practice. The boy explained, "The funeral was yesterday, and tomorrow's the big game, and I've *got* to play in it."

"Just a minute," said the coach. "You know I've never put you in the starting lineup before."

"But if you'll start me tomorrow, Coach, you won't be sorry," the teary-eyed boy said pleadingly.

By game time the coach had softened. Deciding to put the boy in for the first play, he reasoned, *He can't do much harm on the kickoff.*

On the first play, the young player came roaring down the field like a tornado. The shocked coach left him in for the second play. He tackled, he blocked, he passed, he ran. He literally won the game for his team that day.

In the locker room afterward, the puzzled coach asked, "Son, what happened?"

The jubilant, perspiring player explained. "Coach, you never did meet my dad, did you? Well, sir, he was blind. And today was the first time he ever saw me play!"

Theologian William Newton Clarke, waiting for life's sunset call, was told it might be a sad experience for one so vigorous as he had been to come to old age and its inevitable feebleness. But he would not have it so. Full of faith in the brighter future which he was confident Christ had in store for him, he wrote:

> Gone, they tell me, is youth,
> Gone, the strength of my life,
> Nothing remains but decline,
> Nothing but age and decay.
>
> Not so! I am God's little child,
> Only beginning to live.
> Coming the days of my prime,
> Coming the strength of my life,
> Coming the vision of God,
> Coming the bloom and my power.

# ELEVEN
## HOW TO GIVE HOPE TO OTHERS

A FORMER PRESIDENT of Sloan-Kettering Laboratories once told a medical convention, "My father was a country doctor. We now know, scientifically speaking, that he didn't carry a thing in that black bag that would cure anybody. But people got well because he patted them and said, 'You're going to make it.' The hope he inspired released the body's amazing power to heal itself."

One day when King Saul was seeking David's life, Saul's son, Jonathan, searched out David in the woods and encouraged him with these words, "Fear not; for the hand of Saul my father shall not find thee; and thou shalt be king over Israel" (1 Sam. 23:16-17). Assurance of Jonathan's unbroken love and of his own destined occupancy of the throne doubtless revived David's hope and helped him bear his exile.

**Be a Caring Friend**
To give hope to an individual we must befriend that one, showing ourselves to be persons of love and hope. When Jesus

met vacillating, oscillating, impulsive Simon for the first time, He saw what this wavering fisherman could become—solid, stable, firm, and dependable. He gave Simon hope by calling him a rock (Peter).

At an international convention on psychology, a report was made on a study started 30 years previously. Graduate students at Johns Hopkins University had studied 200 young men between the ages of 12 and 16 who lived in an inner-city ghetto, and then predicted how these boys would turn out 25 years later. The graduate students predicted that 196 of the 200 boys would spend some time in jail.

A quarter of a century later another group of college students were told to find the 200 men and check on the predictions. Able to locate 180 of the 200, they discovered that only six had ever spent time in jail. Challenged to discover why the earlier forecasts were so wrong, the college students noted that 75 percent of those men questioned referred to a teacher. Finding this oft-mentioned teacher, the researchers asked her strategy in communicating positive values to these young men. She replied, "I just loved those boys; that's all."

Psychologists reported that in North Korean prisoner-of-war camps, many prisoners were saved from death through the efforts of friends who firmly motivated them toward realistic goals, or reminded them of ties to loved ones at home.

Advisors in bedside manners for hospital visits warn, "No matter what you may know about the prognosis, say nothing that would undermine the patient's hope—a vital ingredient in healing" (Olive Evans, "Bedside Manners," *McCall's*, March 1984, p. 68).


Don't Give False Hope
Israeli psychologist Dr. Shlomo Breznitz, visiting scientist at the U.S. National Institute for Mental Health, made a study on

the part hope plays in helping people recover from illness, cope with stress, or survive disaster. He says hoping is an active process in which one imagines a positive future based on a realistic assessment of the present. He distinguishes four styles of response to trouble. The first—hope based on reality—is the most effective method to manage problems. The second—hope plus denial—rests on illusion, which may result in deniers falling apart when faced with bad news. The third style—total denial—when a person blots out a difficulty totally—is at least a sign that the person is fighting, a psychological vital sign. The fourth reaction—giving up—indicates neither hoping nor denying, and has the poorest prognosis (*Vogue,* July 1984, p. 88).

If a person suffers from some malady, hope of healing should be presented realistically. If the healing occurs, we thank God for a miracle. If the infirmity remains, we realize that God has not failed us, but will use the illness to bring glory to Himself and good to us.

In her book, *On Death and Dying* (Macmillan), Dr. Elisabeth Kubler-Ross says it's possible for a sensitive doctor to make a patient aware of a serious illness without removing all hope from him. Even in cases of terminal illness, the doctor should leave the door open for hope, specifically through new drugs, techniques, and research, communicating to the patient that he is not giving him up because of a serious diagnosis, but that they will fight the battle together, no matter the result.

When someone passes away without making any profession of faith in Christ, we do not wish to give false hope. However, who knows what goes on in the mind of a person in their last conscious moments? A blatant unbeliever, widely known for his atheistic views, was knocked overboard in a storm at sea. Managing to cling to a spar, he was rescued the next day. Immediately he told people, "If I had drowned, you all would've thought I died an unbeliever. But in those moments in the water when I was struggling to keep afloat, I prayed to receive

Christ as my Saviour and became a believer." He proved the genuineness of his conversion by living a godly life in the years that followed.

In an old inn at St. Moritz in the Swiss Alps is an inscription, which translated from the German reads, "When you think everything is hopeless, a little ray of light comes from somewhere."

*Point out the positive side.* Realistic hope stresses the glass is half full, not half empty. During World War II when Allied planes were shot down in large numbers, pilots began to show signs of psychological distress, thinking, *It won't be long before my number is up.* Then top command began the policy of the forty-mission tour of duty, after which pilots could go home. With a definite, limited number of remaining flights, pilots' outlooks changed, increasing their hope. With each successful mission, they knew their chance of survival was higher.

My wife will never forget the answer the late Dr. V.R. Edman, then President of Wheaton College, gave her when she asked, "How in the world will my husband and I ever get our seven daughters through college?" His reply, "If God wants your girls to go to college, nothing in the world will stop them!" Today all seven are college-educated.

We should help someone to fantasize, imagine, anticipate, or envision the good that may yet be. One value of positive thinking is that the greater the perceived probability of reaching an important goal, the more likely will the person move in the direction of its achievement. In his book, *Encouraging One Another,* Gene Getz tells how midst doctrinal confusion, emotional instability, and spiritual immaturity, one of his college professors kept focusing on his positive qualities. Getz says that were it not for the professor's personal encouragement, he would not have made it through the first semester at Moody Bible Institute. God used the professor to shape the direction of Getz's life (Victor Books, pp. 32-33).

## HOW TO GIVE HOPE TO OTHERS

In pointing out the positive to despairing persons, we can remind them that they have the prerogative of choosing their attitude.

*Point out what God has done in the past.* When the Israelites were battling the Philistines, Samuel took a stone, calling the spot where he set it *Ebenezer* ("Hitherto hath the Lord helped us"—1 Sam. 7:12). This reminder of past victories brought hope to the Israelites who then subdued the enemy.

As a member of the Conservative Baptist Foreign Mission Board, my wife rubs shoulders with newly appointed missionaries who face the seemingly impossible task of raising their support in a short period. She often tells them the story of Nancy, a young lady from our church, now a Wycliffe missionary in Cameroun, Africa. In her seminary days Nancy took care of a student's wife who because of a history of miscarriages needed bedrest and care during pregnancy. The couple had little money to reimburse Nancy. A few years later, just before she was to go to the field and in need of more support, Nancy received a phone call from the couple saying they had inherited money and were pledging a sizable amount for her monthly support. This story spurs hope.

We can recommend books to fit needy cases. Parents with children who have been hurt in accidents could derive hope from the book, *Race For Life* (Zondervan), the account of Joel Sonnenberg, who was burned over 85 percent of his body and who has fought back to a good degree of normalcy.

The despairing can be encouraged to select heroes, not only biblical characters like Joseph and Paul, but current victors whose triumphs show us what we can become.

**Share from Your Own Experience**
Jeff Blatnick, the super heavyweight on America's 1980 wrestling Olympic team, was lifting weights in 1982 when he first

noticed small lumps, which turned out to be Hodgkin's disease. Though doctors wanted him to give up training, he kept on. In 1983 he was declared cured and resumed workouts in earnest. In 1984 he won the Olympic gold medal in the super heavyweight Greco-Roman division. Knowing his story can catch the attention of cancer victims everywhere, this winner says, "If I can be an inspiration, that's great." He tells anybody battling a life-threatening disease to maintain as normal a lifestyle as possible.

Some hospitals have initiated programs whereby a person facing surgery can be visited by a patient who has lived through a similar operation. Since hope is such a crucial ingredient in coping with affliction, realistic success stories have a real purpose.

An ex-alcoholic who broke the chains of drink two decades ago says the first step in dealing with alcoholics is to give them confidence. The problem drinker must see he might just make it this time. He gives them his story and God's promises and introduces them to other ex-alcoholics who have won.

The cover of *Essence,* subtitled "The Magazine for Today's Black Woman," carried across its December 1983 issue in red letters the word *HOPE*. The cover story concerned Antonia, a girl born into a ghetto where her father was a pimp and her mother a prostitute, and both drug addicts. She became an incest victim, junkie, drug dealer, and jailbird. Today she is a wife and mother, stately, attractive, owner of a growing private business, and a prison counselor. She inspires inmates telling how she hit back with all the strikes against her. She says, "I am what I am today because of Christ. I owe my success to God and to Walter Hoving Home. How could I have known there was any other life besides drugs and the street?" She tells her story to inspire hope in other women trapped in the same predicament.

A lady, watching her seriously ill husband get weaker and

weaker, related how she had hope of healing almost to the end. Then when she realized he wasn't going to recover, she found that peace replaced hope. Her experience encourages others whose mates may be seriously ill.

### Don't Be a Discourager

William Barclay said, "One of the highest of human duties is the duty of encouragement. . . . It is easy to laugh at men's ideals; it is easy to pour cold water on their enthusiasm; it is easy to discourage others. The world is full of discouragers. We have a Christian duty to encourage one another. Many a time a word of praise or thanks or appreciation or cheer has kept a man on his feet. Blessed is the man who speaks such a word."

Some years ago I suffered minor dizziness from time to time, even finding it difficult to preach on occasion. I mentioned my problem on a visit to my mother. Immediately she responded, "My son, you'll get over it." Subsequent examination revealed a very minor weakness of the middle ear, which solved itself as the months went by. But I recall how in the meantime my mother's words had given me hope.

A youthful preacher in his first church hoped for a congregation of hundreds, but only a handful came. Mentioning his dream to an older pastor and lamenting that he had only a dozen in church the previous Sunday, the older cleric commented, "Don't feel badly. I know a man who had twelve followers and He did all right!"

*Help people set goals.* Parents with a child terminally ill with leukemia, and faced with long-range hopelessness, found that selecting more immediate goals, instead of concentrating on the impossible goal of their child's survival, made their situation more bearable. The hope of reaching a series of short-range goals, like taking their child to the circus, kept them going through the final days of their child's life.

## THE SUSTAINING POWER OF HOPE

*Challenge people to try new things.* People get in a rut, repeating practices which do not work. Suggest a fresh approach. Lead them to brainstorm new ideas. Encourage them to ferret out new avenues, but leave the evaluation and final decision to them.

*Pitch in when help is needed.* As you analyze someone's seemingly hopeless situation, you may conclude the solution requires your active help, and pitch in. In 1983 the *Gordon*, published by Gordon College, carried a feature on Hillary Marides, born prematurely with cerebral palsy. The doctor told her father that it would be a miracle if she lived. She did. Later, they said she would never be able to stand. She stands. They said she could never complete a high school education, but she graduated at the top of her class. They said college was an impossibility, yet when the article appeared, she was a freshman at Gordon.

All this would likely never have been accomplished had not her father sold his successful restaurant business to devote himself full-time to Hillary, and with the help of neurological experts, set up a strenuous regimen of daily muscle manipulation. Sometimes it took six frustrating months to train just one muscle.

When Hillary was in high school, nearby Gordon College students volunteered to help, setting up a demanding schedule of three to four hours of therapy five days a week. Her dream of going to Gordon College was realized. Students reported it impossible to spend time with her and not come away deeply moved by her faith, optimism, and determination. She has been the subject of many local TV shows and newspaper stories.

Hillary says that coping with her disability is tough, and that without her faith and hope in God it would be almost impossible. She has observed the devastating effects on others her age who have been institutionalized, left without hope, and *without family or friends to assist* (*Gordon*, December 18, 1983).

## HOW TO GIVE HOPE TO OTHERS

*Reinforce every successful effort.* As a person succeeds at a task, acknowledge it with praise. Let them know you see growth, and what joy their progress brings. Don't hold back when people do well. Teachers of remedial reading have discovered that many children do not mind the lack of interesting material they have to read, as long as they have success in reading it. Each step of mastery sets the stage for better efforts next time.

### Share Christian Hope

A loved one has come to his last hour. All earthly hope is gone. Only one hope—the Christian hope—remains. This is when we again share the living hope of victory over death through Christ's glorious resurrection. Death will usher the believer into the presence of Christ. Pain and suffering cease. He enjoys the wonders of heaven. At the resurrection day he will receive an incorruptible body, exactly suited to his new kind of existence. Paul, after writing about the changed bodies of both living and dead saints at Christ's coming, concludes, "Wherefore comfort one another with these words" (1 Thes. 4:18).

If a person isn't a believer, we can invite that person to embrace this marvelous hope through faith in Christ. *Leadership* told the story of a 26-year-old, attractive girl named Martha, with no signs of illness, who in April 1983 informed the other members of her hospital therapy group that she had just been told she had contracted ALS, also known as Lou Gehrig's disease. Because her father and uncle had died of the same illness, she knew full well the pattern of degeneration in painful detail—first the attack on voluntary movements, such as control over arms and legs, then on involuntary movements, and finally affecting breathing and causing death.

The next month Martha arrived in a wheelchair. Because her walking had been severely impaired, she had been fired from her job at a university library. By the second month, she had lost the use of her right arm and could no longer use crutches. Another month saw the loss of use of both arms so that she could scarcely move the hand controls on her new electric wheelchair. A pastor's wife devoted much time to helping Martha and learned about the many indignities of her suffering. Curled toes would jam painfully in shoes. Help was needed for every move, like getting dressed or even arranging her head on the pillow. When she cried, someone had to wipe her tears and hold a tissue to her nose.

When the pastor's wife talked about Christian hope, Martha turned her off. Her immediate needs were arms that did not flop and a mouth that did not drool. A painless eternity seemed irrelevant. Any thought of God involved how a loving Deity could do this to her. It soon became clear that the disease would complete its horrible cycle quickly. Martha had to practice breathing with a toy-like plastic machine. Sometimes at night she would waken in a panic, seemingly choking, and unable to call for help.

Martha badly wanted two weeks in her apartment to invite her friends over one by one to say good-bye. Government aid would pay for a hospital room, but would not finance a home-stay with all the intensive care she required just to stay alive. At this time a Christian group, the Reba Place Fellowship, offered the free and loving care Martha needed, adopting her as a project and offering to fulfill her last wishes. Sixteen women rearranged their lives, dividing into various work teams to stay with Martha, bathe her, listen to her complaints, help her sit up, stay with her all night, pray for her, and love her.

These women also explained the Christian hope. Finally, Martha, having seen God's love embodied in these women, gave herself in trust to the One who had died for her, not out of fear, but out of love. She gave her testimony at an emotional church service. The day before Thanksgiving, 1983, her misshapen

## HOW TO GIVE HOPE TO OTHERS

body passed away. But today she is in heaven, someday to have a perfect body (*Leadership,* Spring 1984, pp. 96-97).

What other hope do we have to offer a dying world?

# TWELVE
# HOPE OF HARVEST

THE GOVERNOR OF RHODE ISLAND, able to attend only the early part of a banquet before rushing off to another engagement, reached for a roll, then for a pat of butter. Enjoying the roll, he reached for another. Seeing no butter, he called to a waitress, "May I have another pat of butter?"

She replied, "No."

The surprised governor asked, "Do you know who I am?"

The waitress answered, "No."

He said, "I am the governor of Rhode Island."

She countered, "Do you know who I am?"

When he said, "No," she answered, "I'm the waitress in charge of butter!"

The waitress, possessing a sense of responsibility in her position, wanted to be faithful in the discharge of her duties. The New Testament repeatedly urges of God's servants the traits of faithfulness, persistence, continuance, perseverance, and steadfastness, and at the same time reminds us that we shall be ultimately rewarded.

Thirteen years after I left my first pastorate in a Pennsylvania coal-mining area, I received a letter from a young man, whom I had almost forgotten, and who called himself one of the problem youth in that church. He wrote, "Though we were few in number, we were loud! I recall many times the patience you and your good wife had with us." He reminded me how I had helped him with information on the cults, and had given advice on colleges and seminaries.

Then he updated me on how this "coal-cracker" turned out. After military service and graduation from a state teachers' college, he had risen in the public school system, becoming an elementary principal, and then an elementary supervisor for eight years, along the way earning his M.A. and 21 credits toward his Ph.D. All this time he had been active in church life, but despite a lovely wife and three fine children, he felt something was missing. At a church convention he felt a strong call from the Lord to enter the ministry. In less than a year, he was in seminary and an interim pastor of a church in Philadelphia.

He ended his letter, "I think back many times to the influence you had on my spiritual life. At the time you probably thought that love's labors were lost. However, as you can see, *sometimes it takes a while for results to be seen.*" He went on to pastor other churches, sometimes sharing a dual career with the school system.

Probably most Christian workers can relate similar stories of how years after some ministry was completed, they learned that God had used them to be a blessing in someone's life.

In his letter to the Galatians, Paul suggests this will be the experience of every believer who is faithful in doing his God-given task. "Let us not be weary in well-doing; for in due season we shall reap, if we faint not" (Gal. 6:9). This encouragement contains the concepts of well-doing, weariness, and waiting for the harvest. God promises us a harvest, if we keep on keeping on. If the reaping doesn't come in our lifetime, it will be made known to us in the world to come.

# THE SUSTAINING POWER OF HOPE

## The Doing of Good
Though salvation is apart from works, believers are enjoined to do good works as the evidential outflow of their faith (Eph. 2:8-10; Titus 3:5-8). What particular well-doing does Paul have in mind in Galatians 6:9? The context says we are to restore fallen brothers (v. 1), bear each other's burdens (vv. 2-5), and share material things with the Lord's servants (vv. 6-8).

Extending the concept of well-doing may include all our Christian service—such as serving as a Sunday School teacher or officer, singing in the choir, ushering, visiting the sick, calling on prospects, cleaning up after a church social, repairing or maintaining the church property, and a host of other good works, often unknown and unsung, without which a church could not effectively function.

## The Danger of Weariness
The verb, *to be weary,* means to faint, lose heart or spirit, weaken intention, be faint-hearted, become indolent or discouraged. It's fainting, not physically but spiritually, so that a believer weakens his efforts, relaxes his efforts, and becomes spiritually weak.

Interestingly, Paul seems to be making a pun in Galatians 6:9, involving the words *weary* and *good.* The main part of the verb, *be weary,* comes from the adjective *bad. Well-doing* is literally *the doing of good.* In Greek *good* and *bad* are spelled alike, except for one letter. *Good* is *kalos; bad* is *kakos.* To try to give some feeling for Paul's play on words, we translate, "Don't behave badly while behaving beautifully." Or, "In doing good, don't be bad." How can we do good in a bad way? By doing our Christian service with a weary or discouraged attitude.

*Going through the motions.* A famous museum will not permit its guides to work more than two days a week. Officials feel that too frequent repetition of their spiel turns their presentation into meaningless rote.

At a railroad station a woman noticed a lady driver slumped over the steering wheel of her car—half-laughing, half-crying. The woman approached and asked, "Are you feeling all right?" Came the reply, "For the past fourteen years I've driven my husband to the train station every morning. Today, I forgot him!"

We must beware of spiritual weariness due to treating our Christian service routinely.

*Lack of results.* Sometimes weariness is due to lack of results. We teach Sunday School, sing in the church choir, go visiting, hand out tracts, and nothing seems to happen.

A man gave out tracts on the same corner for ten years, but no one showed any interest. So he quit. Three months later, he returned to the area and saw a young man handing out tracts on the same corner. Approaching the young man he asked, "How long have you been doing this?" The young man replied, "About three months ago a man handed me a tract on this corner. I took it home, read it, and through its message I became a Christian. I came back the next week to thank the man, but he wasn't here. I concluded he must have died and gone to his reward, so I decided to take his place."

In my teens I had a Sunday School teacher who, though illiterate, witnessed consistently for Christ, including regular tract distribution. Twenty-five years later, on a visit to my home city of Hamilton, Ontario, Canada, on a busy shopping night, I noticed a crowd gathered round a man on a busy corner. Getting closer, I saw my former Sunday School teacher handing out tracts. For well over a quarter of a century he had faithfully engaged in this tract ministry. The following Sunday morning in my home church I was introduced to a man who had become a Christian a few Sundays before through a tract given out by my former teacher.

*Different location.* "This is a tough area for Gospel witness. Most of the people here belong to other faiths. This section is known for its hardness and lack of response." Weariness may come because of our seemingly difficult location.

Yet the early church flourished in the hardest of places, the very city where Jesus was tried and crucified. Despite this obstacle, the early church grew to 5,000 and then more (Acts 4:4; 6:7).

*Monotony of task.* Keeping financial records for a church group, transporting a youth group every week, entertaining church groups in your home, preparing to teach a weekly Sunday School lesson, cooking a church meal—these tasks can grind us down with monotony if we don't exercise spiritual caution.

Dyson Hague, a chaplain in an English hospital, visiting a ward of dying soldiers, was asked by a soldier if he would write his Sunday School teacher and tell her he would die a Christian because of her teaching. A few weeks later Hague received this reply, "May God have mercy on my soul. Just a month ago I resigned my class of young men which I had been teaching for years, for I felt my teaching was getting nowhere. Then came your letter, telling how my teaching had helped win this boy to Christ. I've gone back to the superintendent and asked for my class back. May God have mercy on me!"

*Discouragement.* How easily we become discouraged. Discouragement is a person slandering himself: *You're not making a success of your Christian life. Your Sunday School class doesn't listen. You've never brought anyone to church through your visitation. You've never won anyone to the Lord.* And you feel like quitting.

An old legend tells of the devil selling his tools. Though attractively displayed, they were a gruesome lot—malice, envy, lust, and others all spread out, and each marked with a price. Off to one side lay a harmless looking wedge—shaped tool without a price tag. The devil explained, "That's discouragement. It's the most useful tool I have. With its wedge I can pry open a man's heart when I can't get to him with any of the other tools like stealing or adultery. So few recognize it belongs to me. There's no price on it because I wouldn't sell it for any amount."

Someone said, "What we need is not more initiative, but more finish-iative."

### The Promise of the Harvest
When a farmer sows, he expects to reap a harvest at some future time. In the secular world, the doing of a kind act sometimes brings a reward a few months or years later. Roone Arledge, head of ABC's news and sports divisions, recounts how he got his opening in TV. One summer, while working as headwaiter at a historic inn in Chatham, Massachusetts, the hotel was turning away a family who after a long drive had arrived to find the dining room had closed. Arledge offered to wait on them. Before leaving, the grateful father asked his name. Some time later when young Arledge applied for a job at a pioneering TV network, the man in charge of programming looked up and asked, "How's everything at Wayside Inn?" He was the man who had arrived late for dinner. He recalled the kindness of the headwaiter. Arledge got the job.

The believer's harvest will come in its proper time, whether in this life, or in the world to come. The Bible speaks of the harvest in many ways, like shining as the stars forever (Dan. 12:3); a book of remembrance (Mal. 3:16); treasure in heaven (Matt. 6:20); dividends of a hundredfold (19:27-30); gold, silver, and precious stones which have stood the test of fire (1 Cor. 3:12-14). Ecclesiastes says, "Cast thy bread upon the waters; for thou shalt find it after many days" (Ecc. 11:1).

One cause of spiritual burnout is the gap between expectation and actuality. When our devotion to a cause does not produce the anticipated result, a state of fatigue can result. Realizing that delay of fruit may be due to God's providence should alleviate this frustration. We must not become victims of the visible. Rather, we must walk by faith, believing that as we abide in Christ we are bearing fruit. God is at work. Someday He will show us what He has been accomplishing through us.

*Persistence in working for the harvest.* Visiting an inmate of the Federal House of Detention in New York City, I noticed a message framed on the wall. Hoping its contents would help the prisoner, I asked him to copy the message for me, which he did. It read:

> When Abraham Lincoln was a young man he ran for the legislature in Illinois, and was badly swamped. He next entered business, failed, and spent 17 years of his life paying off the debt of a worthless partner. He fell in love with a beautiful young woman to whom he became engaged. Then she died. Entering politics, he ran for Congress and was badly defeated. He then tried to get an appointment to the U.S. Land Office, but failed. He became a candidate for the U.S. Senate, and was badly defeated. In 1858 he was defeated by Stephen Douglas. But in the face of this defeat and failure, he eventually achieved the highest success attainable in life, and undying fame to the end of time.

Paul, who told us not to become weary in well-doing, certainly practiced what he preached. If anyone had a right to get discouraged, it was the Apostle Paul. Despite trials, testings, torments, losses, and crosses, he said, "We faint not" (2 Cor. 4:16). He often used the word *always* in his writings:

> *Always* abounding in the work of the Lord (1 Cor. 15:58).

# HOPE OF HARVEST

*Always* bearing about in the body the dying of the Lord Jesus (2 Cor. 4:10).
Giving thanks *always* (Eph. 5:20).
Praying *always* (Col. 1:3).

David Brainerd reveals in his journal the need of following the path of duty, even in the midst of dark discouragement. He wrote, "I have very little reason to hope that God had made me instrumental in the conversion of any of the Indians except my interpreter and his wife. I began to entertain thoughts of giving up my mission at the conclusion of the present year. I did so purely through dejection of spirit, pressing discouragement. Just as I lost heart . . . revival. God ordained strength out of weakness" (Jonathan Edwards, ed., *The Life and Diary of David Brainerd,* Moody Press). Brainerd will likely discover in heaven a much fuller harvest than he ever dreamed of back in those difficult days.

*Patience in waiting for the harvest.* A parable tells of a poor farmer who thought of a plan to earn more money from his crops. He intended to get his harvest to market well ahead of the other farmers and have all the buyers to himself. After planting the seed, he watched his field very carefully. As soon as a green shoot appeared just above the ground, the farmer clipped off the sprout and threw it in a bag. When his bags were full, he hauled them off to market. How much easier it was to carry this early crop than hauling more and heavier sacks the old way. But when he arrived at the market, no one wanted the clipped shoots, not even for bird feed. As the farmer drove home without making a single sale, he consoled himself that at least he had brought his harvest to market before anyone else!

No farmer in his right mind expects to reap a harvest right away. We cannot pluck fruit before it is ripe and full-grown. Knowing we shall reap in *due time* should help us develop patience.

## Seeing the Total Picture

A missionary goes to a new field, works for seven years, and has no converts. Another missionary comes out to replace the first one, and thousands are won to Christ. Was the first missionary a failure? By no means. The only reason the second missionary reaped was because the first one sowed. In the day of reward, both will be honored. Every influence, every word, every prayer, every kindness that moves a person in the direction of God will not go unrewarded. One sows, another waters, but God gives the increase (1 Cor. 3:6).

A boy gave his testimony on joining the church. A year prior, a visitor had called at his house and invited him to Sunday School. A week later someone from the church gave him a ride. His Sunday School teacher taught him the Word for months. Others in the church witnessed to him. He heard the pastor preach the Word. Who evangelized this boy? All shared in the harvest. Remember—it took four men to bring the paralytic to Jesus (Mark 2:3). In heaven countless believers will discover they had a share in someone's conversion.

Robert Spruance, the field chairman of North Argentina Conservative Baptist Foreign Mission Society, summarized a recent annual report thus:

> The year 1983 was not the springtime of CB work here. Nor was it the harvesttime. It was one of the periods in between, the summertime, the time of green fruit. It would seem nice to be able to pass directly from the aroma and beauty of springtime blossoms to the harvest of ripened fruit. But God has ordained that the longest period of the growing time be that of green fruit with its variegated problems. But growth continues, almost imperceptibly. And then comes the harvest, a time of rejoicing. In the meantime it is given to us to be faithful in facilitating the growth of God's spiritual harvest.

## Surprises at the Harvest

Three high-school boys from Sheboygan, Wisconsin, on a fun weekend in Chicago, found themselves in a USO Center. A zealous Christian man, witnessing to them, asked if they would like to make their decisions for Christ. Not understanding the Gospel, they were somewhat bewildered when told to bow their heads and repeat the words of his prayer. Not used to praying, and recognizing the incongruity of the situation, the boys peeked between their fingers at each other, burst into laughter, and ran from the building.

A year later, one of the boys, hearing Jack Wyrtzen preach in his high school assembly in Sheboygan, kept thinking, *That's what that man back in the USO in Chicago told me.* The student became a Christian and is today a pastor. He makes this observation, "If he's still living, there's a man back in Chicago who, whenever he thinks of that night when those three boys laughed in his face and ran out of the USO, probably mutters to himself, 'What a failure I was that night!' Little does he know that one of those boys has been a Gospel preacher for many years, due in part to the witness he heard that Saturday night. What a delightful surprise he will receive in heaven when he learns about his harvest."

I am firmly convinced that one of the delights of heaven will be the discoveries of how our faithfulness down here in sowing the seed in the hearts of others resulted in a harvest of godly decisions in their lives. Someone will approach us, "It was the way you lived in your home that showed me the genuineness of Christianity and brought me to Christ." Or, "I watched the kind way you treated your sister after she mistreated you." Or, "It was something you said in a lesson when you were my Sunday School teacher that kept me from backsliding."

Because of our steadfastness—not becoming weary in well-doing—people will tell us they became Christians and decided to go to the mission field, did not commit suicide, entered the ministry, dedicated their lives to Christ, or started a family altar. What joyful surprises await us at harvesttime, if we faint not.

> Who does God's work will get God's pay
> However long may seem the day
> However weary be the way.
>
> God hurries not, nor makes delay,
> Who works for Him will get His pay
> Some certain hour, some certain day.
>
> He does not pay as others pay
> In gold or land or raiment gay,
> In goods that perish not, nor decay.
>
> But God's high wisdom knows a way
> And this is sure, let come what may,
> Who does God's work will get God's pay.
> —Author unknown